Royal Rule
Royal Crisis

THE CHALLENGES FACING A NEW KING IN A NEW AGE

ROLAND GOUGH

THE DUNWICH PRESS

FOREWORD

In this book Roland Gough, author of the bestselling ROYAL FAMILY ROYAL SCANDAL, shows why the house of Windsor is still embroiled in a super-storm of negative criticism from the press and public sufficient to sink the entire Royal Family in the very near future. Gough is a journalist who knows his stuff – he interviews royal staff and those in the know, and presents information the reader can use to form his or her own views as to what really goes on in royal circles. He reveals the questionable practices and odd etiquette of a royal pheasant shoot, and what the Metropolitan Police's 'Royalty and Specialist Protection' squad really think about senior Royals. Gough also explores the contentious issue of racism within the Royal family, and shows why Prince Harry felt compelled to take his family to the USA. He delves into the curious private lives of Anne, Andrew and King Charles, and asks whether members of the British republican movement are correct in their assertion that our present monarch is, in fact, the wrong person to be in a position of unchallenged leadership...

ALSO BY ROLAND GOUGH:
ROYAL FAMILY ROYAL SCANDAL

A definitive account of how royal scandals of the past few years have rocked the Royal Family to its very foundations...

Royal Family Royal Crisis – all rights reserved. The author hereby asserts his rights of copyright over this book. No part of it may be reproduced without the written permission of the author. Copyright 2023 Roland Gough / The Dunwich Press

CONTENTS:

CHAPTER ONE: GOD SAVE THE KING!............ 5

CHAPTER TWO: WHAT THE ROYALS CAN AND CAN'T DO............ 12

CHAPTER THREE: ARE THE ROYAL FAMILY REALLY RACIST?............ 22

CHAPTER FOUR: THE LONG SHADOW OF THE DUKE OF EDINBURGH............ 27

CHAPTER FIVE: CHOPPING OFF HEADS............ 33

CHAPTER SIX: PRINCESS ANNE'S ROLE – MORE OF THE SAME?............ 41

CHAPTER SEVEN: PRINCE ANDREW – NO WAY BACK 44

CHAPTER EIGHT: THE ROYALTY AND SPECIAL PROTECTION SQUAD –WHAT THEY *REALLY* THINK ABOUT THE ROYAL FAMILY............ 50

CHAPTER NINE: WHAT REALLY HAPPENS ON A ROYAL SHOOTING DAY............ 56

CHAPTER TEN: AN EXISTENTIAL THREAT – THE PATH OF AUSTRALIA AND OTHER COMMONWEALTH COUNTRIES............ 69

CHAPTER ELEVEN: THE MAGNIFICENT SEVEN – WHAT THEY WILL DO NEXT.................... 78

CHAPTER TWELVE: HARRY AND MEGHAN: BRITISH EXILE – OR AMERICAN FREEDOM?............ 85

CHAPTER THIRTEEN: THE RISING THREAT OF BRITISH REPUBLICANS.................... 101

APPENDIX 1 – OPRAH'S INTERVIEW WITH PRINCE HARRY AND MEGHAN MARKLE............ 110

REFERENCES........................... 164

CHAPTER ONE:
GOD SAVE THE KING!

The King of England is busy behind closed doors. There are big changes afoot. The death of Her Majesty Queen Elizabeth and the new economies planned by Charles III and Prince William have left a pressing problem. Put simply, there are now too many aides and servants for the main working Royals. The departure of Prince Harry and his wife, Meghan, the Duchess of Sussex has also left a surplus of staff and office space (if rooms in Kensington Palace might be so described). Already, by January 2023 227 staff had been made redundant from Royal residences, but there is great anxiety amongst remaining staff as they wait to see where the axe will fall next.

As a Royal advisor from Buckingham Palace has confirmed, the nervousness in royal households is not confined to the staff. Senior members of the Royal Family are increasingly worried too, as to whether their positions as respected leaders of society are safe. The Prince Andrew scandal, the revelations of the Duke and Duchess of Sussex, and even a row over racism in the Royal Family, are issues rocking the very foundations of British society.

And just when the new King Charles was trying to keep a low profile and impress everybody with his quiet, no-fuss, no-scandal style of exercising his kingship, his own son Harry decided to release several explosive revelations that have done the Royal Family's reputation no good whatsoever. The damage that Prince Harry has inflicted – and continues to inflict – on the Royal Family should not be underestimated. It has been interpreted as having suggestions of racism, inter-family bullying and accusations that Prince William and his wife Kate, the Duchess of Cambridge, deliberately fed the British press stories critical of Meghan Markle. These incidents of in-fighting represent a threat of potentially catastrophic proportions to the reign of Charles.

Perhaps the worst aspect of the threat is that it is ongoing and incessant. Prince Harry, in particular, seems to be out to avenge himself against the members of his family who 'wronged him'. Indeed, if the British press is to be believed, his actions have an element of vindictiveness. For example, on the very evening Prince William was awarding the prizes for his much publicised Earthshot competition for environmentally innovative schemes to save the planet, the Sussex's released the first of their dramatic trailers on American TV advertising their coming Netflix series. Their programs lifted the lid on some of the inner workings of the Royal organisation, and were especially scathing of the aides and personal advisors employed by each of the senior Royals. Harry even said, with regard to Meghan, Duchess of Sussex, that there was an 'unconscious bias' among some of them, implying a racially prejudiced attitude.

While he largely blamed the press for hounding his family, he accused the Royal Family of complicity, by encouraging or at least appeasing, a baying pack of royal correspondents. These journalists, Harry claims, are responsible for forcing the Sussex's out of Britain by breaking their agreements not to follow and harass them wherever they went. Both Harry and Meghan speak of the advisers within the Royal Family that actually gave harmful snippets of information to the press that helped turn the public against the Sussex's. They believe that at other times, far from helping Meghan when she was stressed and suffering suicidal thoughts, these same advisors actually told her she would have to put up with the press, and failed to offer her either sympathy or redress.

If the three-part Netflix documentary on the Sussex's (broadcast in December 2022) was a blow to the Royal Family, Prince Harry's book 'Spare' was an absolute calamity. Released on January 10 2023, it contains information on the motive for the Sussex's exodus from England. There are predictions that the book will do what Guy Fawkes couldn't do, that is, blow up the monarchy and constitution once and for all. If his revelations about King Charles and his brother William are to be believed, the suitability of the pair as monarch and heir respectively has to be questioned. He portrays his brother as having uncontrollable tantrums that led to the younger brother being physically bruised, cut and beaten in a violent attack. As for Charles, he comes across as weak, ineffectual and foolish, not to mention treacherous and duplicitous in the way he cheated on Harry's mother, Princess Diana.

Harry claims, in an interview with English journalist Bryony Gordon that he cut 400 of the original 800 pages of the book because there was sensitive information about his father and brother *"that I just don't want the world to know. Because I don't think they would ever forgive me."* Harry said that his book was not written in order to damage the monarchy, but actually to 'save' it. He believes that he has an obligation to highlight how the institution might damage future 'spares', those next in line for the role of king or queen, such as his brother's younger children. However, palace sources have revealed that William is infuriated by these ideas, and stated that his children were not Harry's responsibility.

It is clear that both Prince William and King Charles believe Harry's book reveals far too much private detail about their lives and interactions. Harry even calls William 'my dear brother, my archnemesis', and refers to his 'alarming' baldness and latterly fading resemblance to his mother. This attempt to hurt is followed by a confession of resentment, that during a walk with his father and brother, William asked Harry why he had not come to them if he believed Palace sources were issuing negative press releases to the tabloid press. But Harry believed it was William and Charles themselves who were ultimately guilty of disloyalty, not the other way around. He felt that as members of his family, they should have been pleased with the initial positive response he and Meghan got as working Royals – whereas in reality, Charles' and William's aides issued nuggets of information implying that Meghan was a bully to her staff, and an antagonist of Princess Kate.

In addition, Harry expressed to William a seething resentment over the agreement termed 'Megxit' by the press, that left him and Meghan without money, without bodyguards and refused him even a minor role in the Royal Family if he chose to live abroad. But William merely stated that the agreement was the work of 'Granny', i.e. the Queen, and that he should have taken up his grievances with her.

William told him, 'I swear to you now on Mummy's life that I just want you to be happy.' Harry, however, despite this sentiment, recounts this meeting with bitterness, and was left with the worst of all feelings against his own family, namely that when he most needed help, he was betrayed.

The British press have speculated on the reasons for these incredibly damaging revelations being served up by Prince Harry, and come up with two reasons: firstly Harry's anger at the perceived sleights he and his wife received at the hands of his family, and, secondly, the prospect of receiving millions of dollars. Meanwhile, King Charles and Prince William fume over this washing of dirty laundry in public. One tabloid newspaper claimed, on its website: 'If the Sussex's want to be stripped of their titles, they are certainly going the right way about it.' [1]

Sources claim that Charles certainly is considering whether to take away Harry's title of Prince, and strip him and Meghan of their Duke and Duchess titles. Furthermore, the exiled Prince and his wife may not now be welcomed back in England for the coronation, where they would be an embarrassment and distraction from the true focus of the ceremony – which is to glorify and raise Charles in the eyes of the British people.

As for Charles himself, there is plenty of evidence he is keenly aware of the precariousness of his position. As soon as Queen Elizabeth died, Charles was working hard, out greeting mourners and well-wishers, first at Balmoral, then in London at the gates of Buckingham Palace. There was an element of spontaneity in his many 'walkabouts' in the times up to and just after the funeral, but overall the pattern was emerging, of the new King making himself available, shaking hands, speaking to the crowds, being seen in front of the people. Camilla the new Queen Consort and Prince William and Kate were also shaking hands and thanking individuals in the crowds for their sympathy and good wishes. Thus was the death of the Queen turned into something of a public relations exercise for William and Charles – but should they really have had to work the crowds in this way in the hour of their grief? Without doubt, it revealed the full extent of the senior Royals' insecurity upon the Queen's immediate passing.

And while all the meeting and greeting of common folk might be put down to their providing reassurance and reminding people of the continuity of the monarchy, rest assured, there was a master-plan in action here.

The new monarch himself, his face haggard with grief, was compelled to show the people of the United Kingdom that the status quo would continue, that Britain's constitutional government was still functioning as before, despite the loss of its matriarch.

But the death of Queen Elizabeth II represents more than just the transition of the monarchical powers to her oldest son. The Royal infighting outlined in this book, the feuding and loss of familial loyalty, the battling of brother against brother, father against son, department against department are symptoms of a great malaise in the institution of Royalty.

It is as if, along with the majority of the people, and the greater part of the British Press, that the individual members of the House of Windsor themselves no longer have confidence and surety that their position is safe, secure and unassailable. And they may well be right: as we shall now see, the fragile position of the Royal Family as a mainstay of the constitution has been eroding away for years and years...

CHAPTER TWO:
WHAT THE ROYALS CAN AND CAN'T DO

There are plenty of people who will tell you the monarchy is an essential part of the British Constitution, but there are far fewer who might tell you *why* that is so. If the king's role was suddenly cut out of the political process, why would it matter? Especially when so much of the political life of our monarch is concerned with what he *can't* do.

Here are ten examples of what the king can't do:
1 Speak openly about political matters.
2 Start or stop a war.
3 Appoint anyone to political office (other than automatically saying yes to a political party's choice for prime minister).
4 Order the army to do anything whatsoever (such as seize power).
5 Raise, lower or collect taxes.
6 Make a proclamation which becomes law.
7 Stop a new law being enacted (except very temporarily).
8 Order the execution of a persona non grata
9 Direct his country's foreign policy
10 Marry whoever he wishes (such as a Roman Catholic).

One wonders what Henry VIII or William the Conqueror would make of this situation. The funny thing is, kings before 1640 or so could do any of these things with virtual impunity. Indeed, people thought the king or queen who had inherited the throne should be a strong, decisive ruler – with parliament there only to automatically ratify what the monarch and his or her courtiers had ordered.

But, as Oliver Cromwell and the puritans discovered, if you suddenly chopped off the king's head, it was still possible to make laws and govern a country. The wonder is why we ever restored the monarchy in 1660, if the new kings and queens were to have absolutely no powers whatever. But republicans beware: what the British really like about their monarch is the aura of *nostalgia* and *ceremony*, the harking back to an imaginary glorious past. That is why in 1660 King Charles II was allowed to ascend the restored throne. And that is why King Charles III now reigns in his turn... and why such an extravaganza of pomp and royal posturing will mark the formal coronation.

But his job is not quite secure. While he may not be foolish enough to try to do any of the ten actions above that would end in an immediate Parliamentary order for him to stand down, there are many other things that could, pretty rapidly, cause him to be ousted from office, or at least launch an existential threat.

These include:
1 Showing that he is not BAME aware.
2 Using the wrong language around ethnicity.
3 Offending against LGBT values.
4 Using the wrong language around gender and sexuality.
5 Telling the paparazzi what he really thinks of them.
6 Being caught bullying staff.
7 Being filmed killing pheasants, deer and other wildlife.
8 Being wasteful of environmental resources.
9 Being wasteful of financial resources.
10 Employing members of staff who offend in any of the above matters

The last of these has already occurred when, in the case of Lady Susan Hussey, Lady-in waiting of the Queen Consort, she uttered her notorious 'where are you really from?' lines to Ngozi Fulani at a Buckingham Palace reception. The newspapers immediately seized upon this instance of apparent racism, which led to a storm of hostile social media posts. These made the matter universally known, and the intensity of vitriolic comments against Lady Susan rose to a crescendo in early December of 2022. The avalanche of bad publicity led to Camilla's head of staff immediately sacking the lady in question.

Once again, the reputation Royal Family was besmirched by behaviour unacceptable in modern Britain. The youth of Britain in particular are ready to seize upon these instances and magnify them into a full-scale political crisis. Had the perpetrator of the comments been a member of the Royal Family there is no telling what the incident may have led to. But, on this occasion, it was a senior member of staff who offended, and the damage was limited by her instant dismissal and an apology that appeared in all the newspapers and on all the royal websites and facebook pages.

But, on the subject of damage to the reputation and prestige, by far the greatest threats to the Royal Family come from within its ranks. In effect, *they are their own worst enemies*, and if things do not change, the obvious corollary to the turmoil sweeping through Buckingham and Kensington Palaces is the eventual abolition of the monarchy. Impossible? That is what Charles I thought in

1649, right up to the time he was beheaded by the Puritans for treason...

However, for Charles III all is not lost: just as the British were getting used to singing God Save the *King*, *S*enior barristers with the title Queen's Counsel changed the stationery from QC to *KC*, and Her Majesty's Theatre, Haymarket, London prepared to change its name yet again, a new opinion poll came out in January 2023 with some surprising results:

1 Do you think Prince Charles will be a good king?
Yes 44% No 31% Don't know 25%

2 Should Charles stand down in favour of Prince William?
Yes 41% No 42% Don't know 17%

3 Are there too many paid members of the Royal Family?
Yes 69% No 5% Don't know 26%

4 Do you think Prince Harry has been badly treated by the Royal Family?
Yes 39% No 35% Don't know 26%

5 Has the Duchess of Sussex been badly treated by the Royal Family?
Yes 59% No 15% Don't know 26%

6 Would you prefer a president instead of a king?
Yes 21% No 55% Don't know 24%

7 Is the Royal Family receiving too much of taxpayers'

money? Yes 83% No 9% Don't know 8%
8   Are you a supporter of the Royal Family in general?
Yes 47% No 32% Don't know 21%

9   Are the Royal Family wasting environmental resources?
Yes 67% No 20% Don't know 13%

10   Do you think some members of the Royal family are racist? Yes 35% No 51% Don't know 14%

11   Are the Royal Family people to look up to?
Yes 22% No 63% Don't know 17%

12   Should the monarchy be abolished?
Yes 33% No 55% Don't know 12%
YouPol 15/01/23 [2]

In some ways, the Royal Family might be reassured by the results: only 33% actually want them to be abolished, though an approval rate of 55% is hardly resounding. And 63% do not think the Royals are 'people to look up to'. Furthermore, 35% think the Royal Family are racist – clearly an unsettling number, no doubt raised by the press reports castigating Lady Susan Hussey in December 2022, and the continuing assertions of Harry and Meghan in their many television appearances.

Supporters of the Royal Family in general are shown as 47%, again, not very convincing. Only 44% think Charles will be a good king, and 41% would like William to take over as king.

69% think there are too many paid members of the royal Family, which speaks volumes. With Charles reportedly cutting down on staff and expenses, one wonders if the economies will be sufficient to sway public opinion. With 83% believing too much taxpayers' money reaches the Royals, it is difficult to see dissatisfaction with the high cost of maintaining them changing too much. While the newspapers, TV and social media currently awash with stories of how British citizens are increasingly hard-pressed for money and urged to economise, the last thing citizens want to be reminded of is that the already rich Royal Family received £85.3 million in the form of the Sovereign Grant. In addition, 67% think the Royals waste environmental resources, highlighting another area of resentment.

Aside from these issues of public perception, there are serious political movements afoot, evident in the way the Royal Family is viewed by Scots, Northern Irish and Welsh people. Significant proportions of their populations no longer want their country ruled by an English-based parliament with Charles III the constitutional head.

Scotland's longstanding quest for independence might be brought about by the next referendum, which Westminster is trying to avoid holding. Wales has a way to go before fully half of its voters opt for independence. But in Northern Ireland, with its population greatly displeased with Brexit and its subsequent trading difficulties, there is a growing appetite for union with the south. Though the province was beforehand divided on religious 'sectarian' lines, census figures will soon reveal that the Catholic population of Northern Ireland has overtaken the

Protestants. And some Brexit-weary protestants are also, for the first time, discussing the merits of leaving the United Kingdom. Thus, there is now the strong possibility of a referendum leading to a truly united Republic of Ireland.

Would an independent Scotland keep the monarchy? Latest indications are that only a minority would wish to do so. After all, why go the independence road only to have the greatest symbol of English hegemony still in place? The same is true for Northern Ireland and Wales: independence would pretty much spell the end of monarchy in these countries.

In the Commonwealth, many of the 14 other independent nations who maintain the monarch as head of state are considering change. Barbados, moved to republicanism in November of 2021, just as a royal visit by William and Kate was about to take place. Jamaica and Antigua will most likely follow, with a growing resentment of past slavery and colonialism now permeating the population.

As for 'the white dominions', as they used to be called, of Canada, Australia and New Zealand, they each have their own movements to cast aside the British monarchy. Though only in Australia is the tide of change sufficiently strong to see all ties with the United Kingdom severed in the near future, in the long term the writing is on the wall for Charles. A generation of younger, more politically conscious people in Canada and New Zealand are turning away from anything that smacks of colonialism. They do not have the reverence for the British Royal Family that their parents had. If the British monarchy is to survive as nominal leader over these Commonwealth nations, it is going to take a concerted effort of public relations to 'sell' King Charles as their head of state.

But even in Britain those opposing the Royal Family are causing a commotion. Graham Smith, head of the campaign group Republic, said that contributions for the Republican cause stalled for a few days after the Queen's death. But thousands of pounds in new funds and a lot of engagement on social media started to occur a few weeks after Charles became king. He puts this down partly to Charles' past behaviour, not least a broken marriage to the sainted Diana, and partly the fact that the Queen was a difficult act to follow. Smith says: 'People did get outraged if you said something bad about her.'

But that level of respect certainly doesn't apply to Charles. The fall-out of his treatment of Princess Diana in the 1990s clouds his reputation to this very day. The Netflix series *The Crown*, while full of inaccuracies, served to remind people of how he cheated on the young Princess, and showed how Diana was virtually forced to make her own way, and her own happiness in the world before her tragic end. On screen, Charles was portrayed as a social dinosaur, an awkward, bumbling figure with a duplicitous streak. In contrast to Diana's shy, sweet nature, he is played on as an entitled, rather snobbish character, eccentric and rather awkward.

Camilla's on-screen portrayal also cast her in a negative light. There is humour, compassion even, but ultimately it is the horrendous treatment of poor Diana that people remember. One only has to dip into social media to see that people have still not forgiven her – or Charles – for their secret affair that is perceived as driving Diana ultimately to her death.

One political commentator shrewdly made the link that the British Royal Family itself is seen as a never-ending soap opera. Indeed, the events that *really* happened lend credence to the dictum that truth is stranger than fiction.

As for the future, it remains to be seen if public opinion in Britain, will continue to support the ruling elite enshrined in its constitution. Sweden, Denmark, Norway and the Netherlands are in a similar position, with a king or queen maintained as nominal head of state. It could be argued that Charles III is in a more precarious situation than the continental kings and queens because, having no written constitution, the British king must do everything according to precedent and expectation. This lends a certain insecurity to everything – and it would only take a simple Act of Parliament to cut off the monarch's role completely.

Would we miss the king, were he to be cut out of the political process? Almost certainly not, as the king's signature to laws passed is simply a formality. The Republican Group's view is that a cake without a cherry on the top is still a cake. Does the United Kingdom need its figurative head of state in the twenty-first century? There are two main schools of thought.

Firstly, MATHEW ENGEL of the Financial Times has written:

'The monarchy may never again work as well as it did under Elizabeth II. But it is the best hope of continuing to provide dignity, stability and a sense of self-worth to whatever remains of the United Kingdom, as well as flummery, gossip and

entertainment'. [3]

Secondly, there is the view of the Republican Group, who, after the Labour Party proposed abolishing the House of Lords in December 2022, commented:

'The British constitution is not fit for purpose, it serves those in government more than it serves the public. For that reason it's to be welcomed that Labour is opening up this debate [on the House of Lords]. But the debate must go further, no part of our constitution can be off limits to serious discussion.' [4]

In other words, the British people must seriously consider the future role of the monarchy, and whether to retain a king as head of government. To have a king, or not to have one – *that* is the question...

CHAPTER THREE:
ARE THE ROYAL FAMILY REALLY RACIST?

The question of whether some members of the royal family are racist has been asked many times. Moreover, it has often been suggested that racism has always existed among royal advisors and retainers. At the end of November 2022 proof of this seemed to be heralded by the conduct of Lady Susan Hussey, who hit the headlines after a series of astonishing comments to a black charities boss at a royal reception at Buckingham Palace. The British GUARDIAN newspaper was quick to post the headline:

PRINCE WILLIAM'S GODMOTHER QUITS PALACE OVER COMMENTS TO BLACK CHARITY BOSS

Meanwhile, the DAILY MAIL's online news headlines of 30th November 2022 offered a partial explanation of what had transpired:

PRINCE WILLIAM'S GODMOTHER LADY SUSAN HUSSEY RESIGNS FROM BUCKINGHAM PALACE ROLE AFTER 'QUIZZING BLACK CHARITY FOUNDER ABOUT WHAT PART OF AFRICA SHE IS FROM'

Both newspapers reported that Lady Susan Hussey, 83, was a Lady in Waiting formerly employed by the Queen, but kept on by Queen Consort Camilla. The lady she insulted is Ngozi Fulani, boss of London charity Sistah Space. Fulani was attending a reception held by the Queen Consort as part of the United Nation's 'Sixteen days against gender violence'. Fulani said the royal aide asked her 'where are you really from' after she had told Hussey she was from Hackney. She said she was 'totally stunned' to be asked repeatedly where she was from *in Africa*.

Lady Susan Hussey, 83, later apologised and 'resigned'. In response to public criticism, the Palace admitted that the comments were 'unacceptable and deeply regrettable' and was taking the incident 'extremely seriously'.

Shocked eyewitness Mandu Reid called the questions 'offensive, racist and unwelcoming'. Ms. Reid says she could not believe her ears after hearing the exchange with a member of the Royal Household, in which Ms Fulani was not just asked once but harangued about revealing where in Africa she was from. Ms. Ngozi Fulani had to explain that she was born and lived in the UK – and *still* was not believed!

Despite requests from the press, Ms. Fulani and advisers from Buckingham Palace at first refused to name the royal lady-in-waiting; but her identity was soon brought to light by the tabloid press. Buckingham Palace then released a statement which said:

'We take this incident extremely seriously and have investigated immediately to establish the full details. In this instance, unacceptable and deeply regrettable comments have been made. We have reached out to Ngozi Fulani on this matter, and are inviting her to discuss all elements of her experience in person if she wishes. In the meantime, the individual concerned would like to express her profound apologies for the hurt caused and has stepped aside from her honorary role with immediate effect. All members of the

household are being reminded of the diversity and inclusivity policies which they are required to uphold at all times.'

Shortly after the event, Ms Fulani described her conversation on Twitter. She recounted it thus:
Hussey: "And where are you from, Ms. Fulani?"
Ms Fulani: "We're based in Hackney."
Hussey: "No, what part of *Africa* are you from?"
Ms Fulani: "I don't know, they didn't leave any records."
Hussey: "Well you must know where you're from, I spent time in France. Where are *you* from?"
Ms Fulani: "Here, in the UK."
Hussey: "No, but what nationality are you?"
Ms Fulani: "I was born here and am British."
Hussey: "No, but where do you *really* come from, where do your people come from?"

There the uncomfortable conversation ended, as Lady Susan Hussey was unlikely to accept that the lady could, in fact, be British. Ms Fulani later posted on Twitter that it had been such a shock to her and two of her co-workers that they were 'stunned into temporary silence.'

Mandu Reid, who is leader of the Women's Equality Party, said that the exchange took place as members of the Royal Household were chatting to guests at the reception when this 'really unpleasant interaction', occurred. Ms. Reid, not mincing her words to journalists, reported that she and other guests were speechless, that Ms. Fulani should receive a proper apology, and that those working for the palace needed to receive training.

Eyebrows were obviously raised that Lady Susan

Hussey was a close personal aide to the late Queen Elizabeth over many decades. Questions have been asked about the attitudes and beliefs of Hussey and other senior Royal advisors.

On the subject of possible racism at the Palace, in March of 2021 the BBC's online news platform revealed that only 8.5% of Buckingham Palace's staff are from an ethnic minority. In London, where the majority of royal workers are based, just under 40% of the population is from an ethnic minority. In response to questions on this matter, a senior Palace spokesman said "We recognise we are not where we want to be and we want to improve. Next year's target is 10%." What he failed to admit, however, is that the proportion of employees from ethnic minorities at the other 21 Royal residences is even lower, estimated to be below 5% overall. If these figures are correct, the obvious inference is that either conscious or unconscious bias must be at play when recruiting staff – possibly being exercised by those in senior positions who are making decisions as to who is taken on.

More seriously, in the interview Prince Harry and Meghan gave in March 2021, hosted by Oprah Winfrey, the couple famously revealed that a senior Royal – not an advisor, but one of Harry's close relatives – had asked about the colour of his future baby's skin. This bombshell was one of the greatest shocks of the program, though the identity of the family member was not revealed. Harry said that this person was not the late Queen – which has left the world guessing, some journalists even speculating that it was Charles who asked the question. But Meghan used the pronoun 'them' rather than he or she, implying two or more Royals had been asking the skin colour questions. Furthermore, it has been pointed out too, that Oprah elicited from Meghan that there were *several* conversations between Harry and his relatives about her unborn child's skin colour, rather than a one-off, ill-phrased inquiry. Meghan also said the questioning was about the baby's skin colour *'and what that would mean or look like'*, implying that a non-white baby would present a problem. She also said, regarding talk within the Royal Family about the baby's skin colour and its consequences, 'It was really hard to be able to see those as compartmentalised conversations.'

I leave the readers to draw their own conclusions as to the identities and true inner feelings and attitudes of these unidentified Royal Family members...

CHAPTER FOUR:
THE LONG SHADOW OF THE
DUKE OF EDINBURGH

Right up until his death in April of 2021 the Duke of Edinburgh cut an imposing figure in British society. He had a reputation for being direct, uncompromising and rather curt with those he didn't approve of. He also had a habit of making controversial comments – some of which have been interpreted as being xenophobic, mocking of other countries, or even downright racist. Once again, I leave the reader to decide whether he really did have these unacceptable views. If not, he certainly had a bizarre knack of upsetting diverse people.

In one of his most famous comments, when Prince Philip visited China in 1986, he told British students studying there: *'If you stay here much longer you'll all become slitty-eyed.'*

In 1999, Prince Philip had reportedly asked black politician, Lord Taylor of Warwick: *'And what exotic part of the world do you come from?'*

In 2003, the prince told the President of Nigeria, who was in national dress: *'You look like you're ready for bed!'*

In 2009, the prince asked the twenty-three members of the black dance troupe 'Diversity' who had come to perform at the Royal Variety Performance: *'Are you all one family?'*

Nor were the home nations exempt from his 'humour'. In 1999, while on a tour in Scotland, the prince expressed sympathy with students for being *'unfortunate enough to be studying in Glasgow'.* In 1995, he asked a Scottish driving instructor: *'How do you keep the natives off the booze long enough to get them through the test?'*

In 2010, during a prize-giving ceremony for the Duke of Edinburgh Awards, a girl told him that she had been to Romania to help in an orphanage. He replied: *'Oh yes, there's a lot of orphanages in Romania - they must breed them'.*

An article in the Sun newspaper in April 2021 listed many of what it called 'embarrassing gaffes' uttered by the prince in his 69 years as the consort of Britain's monarch. But 'gaffe' is not the right way to describe these types of comments. A gaffe is made when one accidentally offends a person in a one-off mistake such as mistakenly calling a man's wife his daughter. What came out of the duke's mouth was deliberately spoken. They were probably intended as jokes, but usually involved a degree of insult – to which the cowed victims were unable to reply.

Philip asked a British trekker in Papua New Guinea in 1998: *'You managed not to get eaten then?'*

And he inquired of an Australian Aboriginal elder William Brin in Queensland in 2002: *'Do you still throw spears at each other?'*

He told a young female officer wearing a bullet-proof vest on Stornoway, Isle of Lewis, in 2002: *'You look like a suicide bomber.'*

After looking at the name badge of businessman Atul Patel at a Palace reception for British Indians in October 2009 he said: *'There's a lot of your family in tonight.'*

On a tour of a community centre in London in 2015, Philip reportedly asked a group of female Asian volunteers:

'So who do you sponge off then?'

The Duke also made comments on democratic and social issues, reportedly telling the vicious Paraguayan dictator General Stroessner in 1963: *'It's a pleasure to be in a country that isn't ruled by its people'.*

In 1981, when unemployment in Thatcher's Britain hit three million, Philip opined: 'A few years ago, everybody was saying we must have more leisure, everyone's working too much. Now everybody's got more leisure time they're complaining they're unemployed. People don't seem to make up their minds what they want.'

The Duke has been praised for his devotion to duty, and he certainly did make a lot of public appearances. On his retirement from public life in May 2017, the British media reported that he had undertaken 22,219 'engagements' in his capacity as the Duke of Edinburgh over six decades. But most of these engagements, involving anything from launching ships and unveiling plaques at town halls to having drinks and tucking into banquets, lasted on average an hour.

As pointed out by the British 'Republic' organisation, over 64 years, that comes down to 350 hours a year, less than seven hours a week. For such exertions, Philip was paid the sum of £360,000 a year. But he had little opportunity to spend his earnings, since everything he ever did, from travelling internationally to dining at top restaurants, was paid for by someone else.

Can Philip's bizarre attitudes be excused as being only a reflection of the thinking and attitudes that dominated the British ruling class in the decades of his upbringing? Once again, that is for *you* to decide. But it might be relevant here to look at Prince Philip's background, and also at his, *and* the Royal Family's association with pre-war Germany.

It is sometimes said that King Edward VIII was forced to abdicate in 1936 not because of his decision to marry Wallis Simpson, a divorcee, which at that time was a contravention of the British constitution, but because the two of them were fanatically pro-Hitler at a time when it was obvious that a war with Germany was looming. Edward is said to have taught the six-year-old Princess (and future Queen) Elizabeth the fascist stiff-arm salute. Undoubtedly, Edward, in 1933, did not project the type of image the ruling classes wanted to see in the country's royal family on the eve of a conflict with the Nazis.

Philip, however, was no fan of the Nazis, despite some strong familial connections. A little bit of his family history will explain this statement a little better.

Prince Philip's father, Prince Andrew of Greece and Denmark, a major-general in the Greek army, was the younger brother of King Constantine of Greece and a cousin to King George V of Britain. His mother, Princess Alice of Battenberg, was a great granddaughter of Queen Victoria.

Philip, the youngest of four children to Andrew and Alice, was born in Corfu at the Greek royal family's summer house in 1921. He was sixth in line to the Greek throne. At the age of eighteen months, however, Philip and the rest of his family had to flee Greece after a disastrous military campaign in Asia Minor led by his father and uncle. Whisked away from Corfu by the Royal Navy, the family decamped to

London, and then Paris, where Philip spent the next ten years.

Philip's family in exile were embedded in the circles of German fascism. All three of his sisters married German princes. One, Sophie, married Prince Christoph of Hesse, a Nazi SS member, whose brother, Prince Philipp of Hesse was a member of the SA, Adolf Hitler's original paramilitary group, known as 'stormtroopers'.

Another sister, Cecile, joined the Nazi Party with her husband George Donatus. They were killed in an aircraft crash in 1937. Hitler and Goebbels sent their condolences to the family, while Goering attended the funeral in person. Philip's third sister, Theodora, married Berthold, prince of the Duchy of Baden who served in the German army at the outbreak of World War Two. Philip could also have ended up serving in the German military like his brothers-in-law.

Instead, with his father disappearing with his mistress to play the tables in Monte Carlo, and his mother confined to a psychiatric asylum in Switzerland suffering from manic depression, Philip was sent to boarding school in Britain in 1932. He spent his teenage years in British schools, first in Surrey and then at Gordonstoun in Scotland, where he became head boy. On completing high school in 1938, Philip was taken under the wing of his uncle Louis Mountbatten, later Viceroy of India. Philip entered officer training in a British naval college before joining the Royal Navy in 1939. World War Two was spent on active service in the Mediterranean and the Indian Ocean, vital arteries for the British Empire.

So it was that by the time of his 1947 engagement to

Elizabeth Windsor, heir to the British throne, Philip was set in his ways, a product of old aristocratic families and archaic views of the world. Were his 'gaffes' merely the unwitting expression of the social mores and values of the circles in which he grew up?

Sixty-nine years as royal consort, kept at huge expense by the public purse to lead a life of self-indulgence, seemed only to reinforce Prince Philip's unlikability, and his rude and overbearing manner. What were regarded as outrageous statements by many were the norm in what counts as 'high society' in Britain – the royal enclosure at the Ascot races, the royal box at Wimbledon, the 'coming out' parties of the debutantes, the country hunts, the London clubs, the Oxford and Cambridge boat race, the Henley Royal Regatta, the charity balls and the countless polo matches. It says something about the British monarchy that, despite his unerring ability to offend, Prince Philip was never advised to alter his often offensive public comments. Why? One hopes this was not because his close advisors were rather too afraid of him and his brusque, forthright manner to speak up and offer wise counsel.

One thing is crystal clear, however: given the incredible furore created by the Queen Consort's companion Lady Susan Hussey, as described in the previous chapter, the hyper-sensitive twenty-first century public have a zero tolerance attitude to any form of racial prejudice or national stereotyping. And the question needs to be asked: if the racist or insulting sentiment came from an older person, the product of colonial times, does it make the utterance any more acceptable?

CHAPTER FIVE:
CHOPPING OFF HEADS

A Buckingham Palace source has revealed that the following surplus Royals are due to have their heads figuratively chopped off. Prince Harry, Meghan Markle, Prince Andrew, Sarah Ferguson, Princess Eugenie, Princess Beatrice, The Duke and Duchess of Gloucester, Prince and Princess Michael of Kent, Princess Alexandra...

All these are surplus to requirements, and will not receive money from the Sovereign Grant directly. But whether they will receive money *indirectly,* for example through the purse of King Charles, or by being allowed to live rent-free in a 'grace-and-favour' crown property, remains to be seen.

Which begs the question – how will these Royals survive financially without a hand-out from the Sovereign Grant? Some, like the Duke of Gloucester have income from private estates, his own being at Barnwell Manor, Northamptonshire. But most have no visible means of support, certainly not sufficient to keep them in the style to which they are accustomed.

As for the rents due from those of them living in Crown properties, this remains to be settled. For instance, the Duke and Duchess of Kent live in Wren House, Kensington Palace, London and its annual rent would be in the region of £350,000. Likewise, Prince Andrew lives in Royal Lodge, Windsor and has a part of Buckingham Palace as well, both Crown properties having a combined rental of many hundreds of thousands of pounds a year. Princess

Eugenie lives in Ivy Cottage, a large crown property. Her sister Beatrice lives in Frogmore Cottage, Windsor, estimated rental (if she were ever to pay) of a mere £200,000.

The truth is, none of these axed non-working Royals could afford to pay their rents in Kensington Palace, Windsor, Buckingham Palace and so on without some kind of subsidy from either the Sovereign Grant directly, or from King Charles handing out money which he has received as a grant beforehand. And while certain members of the family have jobs, such as Princess Eugenie, who is director of an art gallery, and Princess Beatrice, who is vice-president of a software company, they do not earn sufficient money to pay rental on all the royal properties they currently occupy.

Ironically, only Prince Harry and Meghan have sufficient millions of their own to pay rental on a large Royal residence – which they no longer require! Prince Harry has received tens of millions from Netflix and from the book deal he signed that saw *'Spare'* climb high into the best-selling lists. How odd that the sequence of events that forced him to leave the comfortable life of a working Royal have now propelled him into being practically the only self-sufficient Windsor. It is a fairly safe prediction too, that he will be featuring in more documentary films and penning more memoirs to consolidate his new-found money-making role as a disgruntled and ill-treated victim of the Royal Family and the British tabloid press.

Harry and Meghan have conveniently, it seems, opted out of Prince Charles' slimmed down Royal working group. That leaves only the magnificent seven of: King Charles, Camilla, Prince William, Kate, Prince Edward and

Sophie the countess of Wessex, plus Princess Anne, to cover the usual rounds of Royal visits, Royal patronages and roles as heads of various military regiments.

One wonders whether the lesson that Britain can survive with only these few 'working' Royals might lead to demands for further cuts. Perhaps a nation struggling with debt and cost-of-living problems can make do with *one* Royal – i.e. the king. And, taking this one step further, perhaps Britain might be better off with *none* at all – appointing an honorary president to take up a ceremonial post. Is this possible, or likely? The following statistics throw more light on the probabilities of the Royal Family being abolished altogether. They come from a YouGov poll taken a few weeks after the Queen died, a period that saw a great deal of sympathy for the new king.

The November 29 2022 Yougov poll found that 32% of British people thought Charles III would make a good king. 60% were favourable to monarchy but of these only 20% were *very* favourable. This left 40% unfavourable to Charles as a king, of which 20% were *very* unfavourable.

However, 73% in thought he'd provided good leadership after the Queen's passing. Of these, 46% thought he's given *very* good leadership, while 27% believed he'd shown *fairly* good leadership. This gives him some kind of positive platform from which to continue his kingship. Things were not always looking so rosy for Charles. As Prince of Wales he was outspoken about several issues that were important to him, such as the environment and architecture. Indeed, this willingness to intervene in the public space is what led many royal watchers to suspect he would prove a different kind of monarch in the first place, given his mother's studious neutrality on all things. But so far he has kept his views to himself, and followed protocol by not intervening in any political debate or issue.

Despite the warnings from political commentators, it seems that Britons generally wouldn't mind if he *did* intervene. 53% of the public thinks it would be appropriate for the King to publicly express his thoughts on matters that he cares about, according to a YouGov poll of 11 September 2022. However, 35% thought he should retire at some point. 57 % said they were likely to watch the coronation on TV. Surprisingly, 49 % thought Charles should have attended the COP27 summit in 2022, though he was castigated in the press for suggesting he wanted to go.

As for Camilla, 39% were content that she had been awarded the title of Queen Consort. But only 22% thought she should be titled 'queen' as a single word title.

Most of these statistics bode well for the new King and his Queen Consort. Charles and his advisors continue to plan and engineer the new-look Royal Family into something they think the British public will accept. One important decision to be decided is where the Royal couple will live. By November 2022 advisors said that he intended to remain at Clarence House as his principal London address, with plans to move into Buckingham Palace put on hold. With extensive building work and renovations going on at a cost of tens of millions, this is understandable. He has continued using Windsor Castle intermittingly and Sandringham for his Christmas-New Year holiday. It is also expected that Balmoral will still be used as before, with a long stay scheduled for summer of 2023. But Charles also knows that sooner or later he will have to spend at least part of his year at Buckingham Palace, the traditional main residence of the reigning monarch and headquarters of his inner circle of advisers and courtiers.

As stated earlier, Buckingham Palace has seen huge cuts in the number of royal advisory staff, and servants too, as those surrounding the Queen were laid off. One report has suggested that parts of the Palace will soon be open all the year round for tourists, though the greater part of it will still be off-limits. Tourists will not be allowed to use any of its one hundred and seven toilets. These are reserved for Royals and their staff. Of course, these are strictly segregated, so that servants don't use the ones reserved for the Windsors.

As for the toilets for tourists, they are portable loos conveniently hidden away in the gardens and yards *outside* the palace.

Buckingham Palace, though being renovated, is still used on occasion for state functions. For example, in November 22, 2022 a state banquet for South Africa president Cyril Ramaphosa was held, the South African entourage numbering some 160 guests. There Charles hosted the banquet, welcomed his guests and spoke to Mr. Ramaphosa at the dining table and reception held beforehand. Quite whether these sumptuous affairs are strictly necessary for consolidating international relations is open to debate. If they *are* necessary, it can be argued that King Charles is the best person to host this type of event, being politically neutral and untainted by any known views on international events pertaining to Commonwealth countries.

But is Charles setting out on the right foot as a new and modernising ruler? Critics from within the Republic group are sceptical. This is a more challenging time, they maintain, and Charles at 72 is unsuited to serving modern Britain. People are more questioning of authority and resentful of privilege. The king is old fashioned, out of date, left behind by the youth of Britain. The public school education, a place at Trinity College given solely because he was heir to the throne, and a navy commission leading to command of a minesweeper show how he was given an easy passage through life because of his status. His youth spent pursuing beautiful women, leading to the fateful courtship and marriage to Diana Spencer culminated in a sham of a marriage. The duplicitous rekindling of his relationship with Camilla Parker Bowles is now highlighted forever in the Netflix series The Crown. Being in the public gaze is undoubtedly very difficult, but the question needs to be asked as to whether Charles really is a person to look up to, a figure to admire as a leader of the United Kingdom.

His habit of writing to ministers, advocating various political policies and viewpoints was one of the most controversial of his activities during his time as Prince of Wales. It has long been argued that the constitution should have a separation of the sovereign and legislature even to the extent that an heir to the throne should not give advice or push forward an agenda to members of parliament.

Before becoming king, climate concerns occupied a great deal of his time, even before these issues were prominent and in the full focus of political leaders of the world. It could be argued that the worldwide debate on green matters benefitted from his public speeches and lobbying to governments and big business. Undoubtedly, the fact that so high profile a person was highlighting environmental issues contributed immensely to shifting mainstream media attention to these vital areas. But, critics have pointed out how ironic it was that a man who makes a giant carbon footprint and lives a thoroughly privileged life of conspicuous luxury should tell others how to recycle waste products, travel less in aeroplanes and conserve fossil fuels. However, his motives are genuine enough, even if the hypocrisy of advocating one thing but doing another is rather lost to him. For instance, Charles once took a helicopter flight to Cambridge to attend a conference on the reduction of air traffic emissions.

The Republic debate often points to the hypocrisy of a privileged king asserting that everyone else should change their habits. But, as every true environmentalist knows, the first thing one does when attempting to save the planet is to look at one's own carbon footprint and lifestyle.

Critics have also suggested that he might address not only his extravagant and self-indulgent lifestyle, but also his considerable ego – biographer Tom Bower points out that Charles was hugely jealous of Diana's popularity, for instance. Prince Harry also thinks that Charles resented his wife Meghan stealing the royal limelight, too.

There are other niggling concerns that point to Charles being somewhat peculiar in character. His valet reportedly irons his shoelaces every day, has to squeeze the right amount of toothpaste on the royal toothbrush, and gets shouted at if the King's several changes of clothes are not laid out ready for him each day. More seriously, Palace aids are said to be wary of the temper tantrums that allegedly occur when his expectations are not met.

And so, the question has to be asked: can a rather odd, white, extremely privileged male aristocrat really exert leadership over an ethnically diverse, financially challenged country? Is Charles really the constitutional head of state twenty-first century Britain requires? And if the electorate were to choose a suitable person to act as ceremonial figurehead of the United Kingdom, would Charles be seen as an acceptable choice? A comment placed below the YouTube video 'Could Britain End the Monarchy & Become a Republic?' posted by TLDR News reads as follows:

'All things considered, the idea of Charles being chosen as a leader of the country is, quite frankly, laughable.'

CHAPTER SIX:
PRINCESS ANNE'S ROLE – MORE OF THE SAME?

Princess Anne is patron of over 300 organisations, including Riders For Health and the Carers Trust. Her charity work revolves around sports, sciences and people with disabilities and health in developing countries. She has been associated with Save The Children for over fifty years and has visited a number of their projects. She has over forty military ranks and appointments.

If ever justification was sought for a Royal Family member being paid out of the Sovereign Grant, Anne is the one to look to as delivering 'value for money'. She has been called the Royal Family's most reliable member, having carried out over 20,000 engagements since her 18th birthday. The media often called the young Anne 'aloof' and 'haughty', and reported instances of swearing at members of the press. She told photographers to 'naff off' at the Badminton Horse Trials in 1982. *Vanity Fair* wrote that Anne 'has a reputation for having inherited her father's famously sharp tongue and waspish wit'. She says of her work: 'It's about serving... it took me probably 10 years before I really felt confident enough to contribute to Save the Children's public debates because you needed to understand how it works on the ground and that needed a very wide coverage. So my early trips were really important.'

Reportedly, Anne insists on doing her own make-up and hair and drives herself to engagements, having pleaded guilty to two separate speeding fines on account of being late. She does not shake hands with the public during walkabouts, saying, 'the theory was that you couldn't shake hands with everybody, so don't start!'

Her reputation is also coupled with her advocacy for causes out of the mainstream, such as the Wetwheels Foundation's commitment to accessible sailing, and the National Lighthouse Museum. On her 60th and 70th birthdays, the BBC and *Vanity Fair* both asked whether she would retire, and she denied it both times, citing her parents' example as well as her commitment to her royal duties.

Anne's public personality has been described as 'not suffering fools lightly' and members of her staff have reportedly been given the sharp edge of her tongue for not performing duties diligently or on time. Anne is the patron of U.K. Fashion and Textile Association. She has been noted for wearing British clothing brands of a country-gentry style, Her style choices often reflect her equestrian interests as well as the practicality of her fast-paced schedule. Anne has appeared on three British *Vogue* covers. She was featured in the cover story for the May 2020 issue of *Vanity Fair*.

Anne is the only member of the royal family to have been convicted of a criminal offence. In November 2002, she pleaded guilty to one charge of having a dog dangerously out of control, an offence under the Dangerous Dogs Act 1991 and was fined £500

While speculation grows over what exactly her husband and children are doing, Anne quietly continues with her royal duties. Almost the perfect royal – hard working, quiet as far as talking to the press is concerned, a family orientated person, rarely criticised apart from the 'sin' of divorce.

She was, however, criticised for going to Falkland Islands in November 2022 by the Argentine government, much to the delight of the British press. The Sun newspaper reported that 'no sleep will be lost by Anne, or anyone in the British government or military because of that visit.'

Her future role is likely to be more of the same kind of royal visits and public duties. If her role was to be censured at all, it must be from the viewpoint that the Royal Family itself should not be used as an institution to figurehead military regiments and units, charities and other organisations. However, the question arises as to whether such a no-nonsense hard-working role could be formulated by simply *paying* a large salary to an individual to do the same kind of leadership-patronage roles.

Princess Anne, more than any other Royal Family member, seems impervious to criticism, and heedless of what the press and public make of her. In a nutshell, her attitude to work is that she just 'gets on with it' and shuns all forms of self-aggrandisement. The other Royals would do well to look at her track record and follow her example.

CHAPTER SEVEN:
PRINCE ANDREW – NO WAY BACK

If there was one Royal who might be used to contrast Princess Anne's no-nonsense, low profile attitude to royal life, it would be the haughty, abrasive, always-in-trouble Prince Andrew. One royal source has said that the prince, due to his notoriety, may be asked to leave his apartment at Buckingham Palace, sometime in 2023. If so, his fall from power and grace will be almost complete.

Almost but not quite: a parliamentary bill is being prepared for 2023 that will strip him of his Dukedom and other remaining titles – reducing him, in effect, to the rank of a commoner and without even a stipend to pay for his lavish lifestyle.

Even so, he reportedly still has hopes of returning to public life. While Queen Elizabeth was alive he is said to have asked her to restore him to his royal duties. But both King Charles and Prince William are said to be absolutely opposed to his ever re-entering public life as a working royal. Effectively, Andrew has been banished from public life, though he won't be sinking into obscurity without a fight.

When, in January 2023 Ghislaine Maxwell said in an interview that the notorious photograph of Andrew and Virginia Giuffre was a fake, there were indications the prince might get his legal team to overthrow the legal settlement that had cost him £12 million. But advisors of King Charles and William, according to press sources, moved rapidly to stymie this attempt before more adverse publicity was heaped on the head of the 'Pariah Prince'. The last thing

Charles and William wanted was the resurrection of the press furore that accompanied the Virginia Giuffre lawsuit launched against Andrew in early 2022 that was, to put it bluntly, a public relations disaster for the Royal Family.

On a minor note, Andrew was even said to be angry at being ignored during the 40 year commemorations of the 1982 Falklands War in April and May of 2022. One wonders when his new reality will finally dawn on him, that he is considered a public relations liability, an ever-present embarrassment and a walking reminder to all of the unacceptable side of royal privilege.

There is one more great humiliation that could befall him, namely his exclusion from the line of accession to the British throne. For, Prince Andrew, Duke of York, is eighth in the line of succession and the first person in the line who is not a descendant of the reigning monarch. Considering Andrew as a future king, of course, is a very theoretical matter, unless some kind of disaster occurred such as the balcony of Buckingham Palace collapsing while the entire new royal order (minus Andrew) were on it. Disasters apart, it is still irksome to many that Andrew is even in the queue for accession, and therefore it is quite possible king Charles may decide to complete the whitewashing of his clan by finally stripping Andrew of every last vestige of royalty, and push him out into the cold, cold world of ordinary citizenry. How are the mighty fallen! The fact that Andrew served in the Royal Navy as a helicopter pilot during the Falklands War and was considered something of a hero is no longer sufficient reason for the press to accord him any respect whatever. He has been vilified, criticised, pilloried and hung out to dry. Nor is his family much more welcome, either.

With Sarah Ferguson he has two daughters: Princess Beatrice and Princess Eugenie. Andrew and Fergie's televised marriage, followed by the media frenzy pursuant to their separation in 1992, and divorce in 1996, certainly put them in the public eye, though not in a good way. As Duke of York, Andrew undertook official duties and engagements on behalf of the Queen. He served as the UK's Special Representative For Trade for 10 years until July 2011 when he left under a cloud. His appointment in the first place was controversial, as Andrew was said to be a friend of Saif al-Islam Gaddafi, son of the late dictator, and also a pal of the convicted Libyan gun smuggler Tarek Kaituni. Problems arose when he hosted a lunch for Sakher El Materi a member of the corrupt Tunisian regime at the Palace around the time of the Tunisian Revolution. Andrew also formed a friendship with Ilham Aliyev, the president of Azerbaijan who has been linked with various corruption scandals, of which Andrew has denied any knowledge.

Andrew left the post when the Jeffrey Epstein scandal became more widely known in 2011. His associations with Epstein proved to be by far the most damaging blows to his reputation and royal standing. The details are fairly well known, that he was a friend of Epstein from the 1990's, and was said by Virginia Giuffre, a victim of sex trafficking, to have had sexual relations with her on three occasions. Despite his denials and rejection of her accusations, he nevertheless paid her a multi-million pound sum (said by the press to be £12 million). This move was widely seen as tantamount to an admission of guilt, though legally, of course, it is nothing of the sort.

The Royal Family itself certainly seem to be treating Prince Andrew as if he were guilty. And, so far as the public are concerned, Andrew is a pariah to be pilloried and ridiculed on social media and even booed when seen in public.

The late Queen Elizabeth, perhaps prompted by her son Charles and grandson William, saw fit to take away most of Andrew's titles and ceremonial appointments in January 2022. Andrew's social media accounts were deleted, and his page on the royal family's website was rewritten in the past tense implying he was no longer a full member of the royal family. Dozens of his military affiliations and patronages were removed. He was also stopped from using the style His Royal Highness (HRH). By this time he had already been expunged from his roles as patrons of about a hundred charities and NGO's.

Andrew continues to be ridiculed and heavily criticized on social media and by the mainstream press. Royal aides have indicated that Andrew is still something of an embarrassment and dark shadow in the new era of King Charles III. He is, while still in Buckingham Palace, and while still harbouring hopes of some kind of comeback into public life, something of a festering wound in the British monarchy, even with him geographically, financially and socially excluded from the 'modernised' form of royalty that Charles is said to be instigating. But public memory is long, and posts on social media cannot be whitewashed off his record – and his record is, in the public's view, still inextricably linked to that of his brother the king. Thus, the wayward Prince still besmirches the reputation of the House of Windsor.

King Charles even dealt his brother the killer blow – perhaps literally if things go awry – of taking away Andrew's armed protection squad. These policemen cost the taxpayer about £3 million a year, and have long been a controversial matter for several reasons. The expense of having round-the-clock officers dragged around the country, *and* the world, even for skiing trips and visits to golf courses did not sit well with the media and public. Whether Andrew remains a target for terrorists or hostile foreign powers is open to debate. While he may be rather a soft target without protection, and an unimportant one as the outcast black sheep of the royal flock, it seems a little cruel to suddenly strip him of his Protection Squad officers. Reportedly, however, the police themselves are jubilant about no longer having to accompany the prince wherever he goes.

While no serving officer was prepared to comment, Dai Davies, a former chief superintendent who formerly led the Metropolitan's Royalty Protection unit, said that the money used to protect the Royal could instead be used to solve thousands of crimes in London. 'Why should we pander to this over-inflated egotist called Andrew?' he said. Davies was previously the Operational Unit Commander in charge of royal protection for the late Queen and the Royal Family in 1995. He was formerly responsible for Palace and Personal Protection throughout the UK and worldwide.

Perhaps significantly, Andrew has been seen on several occasions driving himself in a range rover around Windsor Park and the nearby town centre, which the press speculated was in preparation for his impending new life without his officers driving him. There was yet more speculation that his residence of Royal Lodge could also be taken from him, though as he paid over £5 million for refurbishment and renovations the Crown Estates management might adjudicate that he is allowed to remain rent-free, at least for the time being.

One tiny life-line was recently cast to him. In November 2022 it was made known to the press that Andrew and Sarah Ferguson were invited to attend Sandringham at Christmas. Ferguson was hitherto banned from royal festivities in Norfolk by the Queen, following a storm of bad publicity in the 1990's alleging various infidelities while still married to Andrew. The very fact that Andrew and Ferguson (now the best of friends again) have been allowed in from the cold may show that despite the harsh measures meted out to Andrew from the late Queen, King Charles and Prince William still consider him 'one of their own'. Perhaps, when all is said and done, royal blood is thicker than water.

CHAPTER EIGHT:
THE ROYALTY AND SPECIAL PROTECTION SQUAD – WHAT THEY *REALLY* THINK ABOUT THE ROYAL FAMILY

The Royal Family are guarded by armed officers of the Metropolitan Police's 'Royalty and Specialist Protection' (RaSP) department which was formed following a merger of the Royalty Protection Command (SO14) with the Specialist Protection Command (SO1) in April 2015.

The department has three service areas, which are:
Close Protection – which offers members of the Royal Family, government ministers and visiting heads of state armed officers to guard them.
The Special Escort Group (SEG) who provide mobile armed protection to members of the royal family and government ministers.
Armed Security which gives armed protection to occupants of royal residences in London, Windsor and Scotland.

These police officers, while working in close proximity to members of the Royal Family, are not to be confused with royal employees. They are independent policemen who do not like to be treated offhandedly or without common courtesy. After all, they are in a position where they may have to risk their lives to protect VIP's.

However, according to a number of officers, some Royals – such as Prince Andrew – have nevertheless abused and disrespected individuals of their own allocated protection team. This didn't go down very well with Metropolitan officers in question. From the various interviews they have given, and their social media posts, particularly on YouTube[5] it has become pretty obvious over the last few years that the Metropolitan police Royal and Specialist Protection squad members do not buy into the idea that they're protecting their 'superiors'. While one officer called Prince Andrew an 'over inflated egotist' from the films posted on U-Tube by ex-members of the group, it is doubtful they have much higher opinions of any other member of the Royal Family.

Royal security officer Paul Page has spoken out on life inside the Royal Family. Prince Charles, he says, was not the most popular of individuals in the Royal Family among the protection officers because of what had happened to Princess Diana – they considered it was his fault. While Princes Harry and William were polite and friendly, and most members of the household were civil, Prince Andrew was 'obnoxious, and an angry individual'. He would 'fly off the handle' with maids, footmen and policemen alike. Paul Page recounted the story of a maid who was shouted at for not arranging Andrew's 72 teddy bears in the correct place on a bed. He also recalled being sworn at for not letting in one of Andrew's female guests without the proper authorisation.

Furthermore, on many occasions around the year 2000 the now jailed Ghislaine Maxwell visited Andrew in Buckingham Palace, but the officers were told not to put her name in the visitors' book. Officers believed she was in an intimate relationship with the prince, so frequent were her trips to see him. No other guest was given virtually carte blanche to access his apartments. Page also recalls being abused with four letter words when they believed there was an intruder in the Queen's rooms and found Andrew padding about in the corridors. Officers were extremely upset at being cursed in the course of their duties, and lamented how their procedures were frequently broken or challenged by Andrew's habit of telling guests to come to his rooms without informing the Royal Protection officers beforehand. All in all, they branded Andrew something of a security nightmare, and a very objectionable fellow to boot.

Page also spoke of how, after the intruder Michael Fagin got into the Queen's bedroom, security was ramped up. Laser beam alarms, pressure pads and CCTV covering all royal residences were set up. Officers were assigned to sit outside royal bedrooms all night. Officers were also cognisant that an attempt had been made to kidnap Princess Anne and that an officer had been shot, but not killed, on that occasion. Therefore, officers are not appreciative of members of the Royal Family – Andrew in particular – making things more difficult for them by not following the protocol that involved telling the police exactly who was entering or leaving royal residences. This certainly highlights just how lacking in privacy is the life of a Royal, and how dependent senior Royals are, night and day, on the RaSP squad officers.

This is confirmed by Simon Morgan, former Police Protection officer for the late Queen, and Charles when he was Prince of Wales. In contrast to Prince Andrew, the Queen was polite and had time to engage and chat about security, as well as other matters. He believes that 21st century security will be enhanced and modernised. For example, at the Queen's funeral, he revealed that armed officers and security personnel were out in maximum strength, even mixing in with the crowds, in order to deal with possible threats.

Morgan speculated on how Harry and Meghan's security would prove very challenging once they left Britain. Private security, rather than police security, would mean having no armed guards when in Britain. However, in the USA this would not be an issue, as security firms employ guards who have permits to carry concealed weapons.

Harry and Meghan's safety during home life would be straightforward enough, Morgan believed, but travelling around the world would be very problematical and costly, to the tune of $20 million. Officers or agents would need to travel in advance, be on call 24 hours a day, and work in shifts. Skilled ex-police or military men and women 'don't come cheap' Morgan says. Furthermore, brave individuals who are literally prepared to stop a bullet for an employer, or deal with an armed assailant by returning fire, are special individuals much in demand by the rich elite. No wonder Harry and Meghan lamented the loss of their very experienced – and free – Royal and Specialist Protection officers when they decamped to Canada, and subsequently to the USA.

On the subject of police protection, Harry and Meghan faced 'disgusting, real threats' from far-right extremists, says ex-police chief Neil Basu. Neil Basu who was until recently the force's Assistant Commissioner of Specialist Operations, said teams from the force investigated and prosecuted people behind the threats. Asked in an

interview with Channel 4 if the threats were credible, the police chief, who retired in 2023 after 30 years in the force, said: 'Absolutely, and if you had seen the stuff that was written, and you were receiving that kind of rhetoric that is present online... you would feel under threat all the time.'
Asked if there had been a genuine threat to Meghan's life, Mr Basu, said: 'We had teams investigating it, and people have been prosecuted for those threats.'

The Duke and Duchess of Sussex, who stepped back from frontline royal duties in 2020, now live in California with their two children; and while they have new security personnel in place, the level of protection is not considered to be as formidable as that provided in the UK. The Duke, who is fifth in line to the throne, is suing the Home Office over its decision not to grant him police protection after he decided to leave the UK in 2020.

In the UK, the problems facing police protection officers in the future will be greater, say officers, because Royals like Charles, Camilla, William and Catherine like to meet individuals in crowds, and chat, shake hands and accept gifts. This presents a much more difficult task than simply avoiding threats at scheduled events such as visiting hospitals, schools, government departments and the like where the environment is more predictable and controlled. The ease with which a terrorist or mentally challenged individual could get close to a senior Royal during a walkabout is plain enough to see. Most members of the public are adoring fans, but it only takes one terrorist or deranged person with a knife, a gun or a bomb to be in the front of a crowd in order for a tragedy to occur.

Officers were nervous and on their guard during the interactions leading up to the Queen's funeral, when Charles and William in particular went face to face with the masses of mourners in the street. Thus were the King and his heir both thrust into possible danger at the same time, creating a security nightmare. And it seems likely too, that they, and other members of the Royal Family will be even more 'touchy-feely' with the public in the future. With senior Royals increasingly in very vulnerable and potentially dangerous positions, it may just be a matter of time before one of the crazed kind of individuals who police chief Neil Basu was hunting turns up in person to do something unspeakable. In the final analysis, the only thing averting a tragedy is the dedication and bravery of a few stalwart men who are prepared to put their lives on the line.

CHAPTER NINE:
WHAT REALLY HAPPENS ON A
ROYAL SHOOTING DAY

If the Royal Family are to survive as an institution, the first thing they need to do is give up shooting and hunting wildlife.

Most members of the public are horrified by the violence that sees wildlife shot for pleasure, not least because of the way a large percentage of the quarry are wounded by lead and steel shot. About three in every ten birds shot are hit but not killed by the 240 or so lead pellets blasted out by each cartridge fired from a double barreled 12 gauge shotgun as used on a typical shoot. A degree of cruelty necessarily permeates every single shooting party that takes place. A typical shooting day might see 100-300 birds shot, consisting of pheasant, grey and red-legged partridges, grouse, snipe and woodcock. That means every event sees many birds wounded, and although retrieving dogs pick up most of them, as many as one in ten are never found, but die a slow and painful death from their injuries many hours or even days later.

Gamekeepers and estate workers often observe birds hopping on one leg days after a shoot. Furthermore, up to 150,000 pieces of toxic lead shot are sprayed over the countryside during a typical day's shooting, particles that frequently find their way into the guts of hundreds of non-target species such as small birds, badgers, rodents and even invertebrates such as worms. No wonder a cloud of secrecy shrouds the real goings-on on royal shooting days.

So, what really happens on a royal shooting expedition, when the male members of the family get loaded shotguns in their hands, and pheasant, partridge, woodcock and grouse in their gun-sights?

I asked Robert Benson, a regular at royal shooting bashes to describe a typical day on a shoot. The one he describes took place a few years ago, when the elderly Queen and Duke of Edinburgh attended a day's shooting in Suffolk.

THE AUTHOR: "Bob, you are a veteran of attending Royal shooting parties, I wonder if you could describe one of these, in as much detail as possible, please."
BOB: "I remember standing next to Her Majesty the Queen at Helmingham, as a hundred and fifty yards to our front the eight guns of the shooting party were blazing away at pheasant, woodcock and the occasional partridge. Her Majesty, like myself, had a job to do, picking up the shot birds with retrieving dogs, an occupation that gave a good view of the day's action. Not many people know that the Queen employed a full-time dog trainer at Sandringham to breed, train and transport her labrador retrievers. At any one time she might have had a dozen ready to use on her Norfolk estate, or take to Balmoral and Windsor, or sometimes to other sporting venues where the Royals were invited to shoot game. On these days, while the male members of the family were shooting, the Queen's greatest pleasure was to pick up the fallen birds with the regular dog-handlers like myself.

Helmingham is one of the places where I used to see the Royal Family several times a year. On the day I'm describing, Prince Philip was amongst the guns, along with

Princes Charles, Andrew and Edward, and the day was hosted by their relative and close friend, Lord Tollemache. There were three other guns, too, other relatives, most probably, whom I didn't recognise.

On the first 'drive', which is what we call the flushing out of birds from a covert by the beaters, we stood waiting for the game to begin flying over the guns. The Queen was dressed in a long brown Barbour jacket, green wellington boots and a tartan headscarf. We both had two black labradors sitting in front of us, and both of us have the same kind of black dog-whistles round our necks, the kind professionals use, and similar walking sticks too, finished with carved deer antler at the top end. There are certain kinds of clothing and equipment used on virtually every shoot. I guess it's become part of the etiquette surrounding game shooting over the years. As I said before, I reckon we were a hundred and fifty yards behind the guns, waiting to pick up the birds that fell onto the grass.

Twenty yards behind us, leaning against the queen's own green land rover was her personal bodyguard, a police royal protection squad officer. I knew that he was armed with a pistol in a shoulder holster because you could see a bulge in the left side of his chest beneath his own brown Barbour jacket. Anyway, he didn't help or participate in any of the day's sporting activities, he was just a spectator and to be honest he looked rather bored. He didn't even drive the vehicle, because on shooting days it was Her Majesty's delight to drive herself around the various estates.

A range rover with two more armed policemen was parked at the far end of the shooting line, the same distance back from the shooters as we were. Whereas we were standing on the open grassland, they were parked on a gravel driveway, which led behind them to the rear entrance of Helmingham Hall park. The whole park consists of several hundred acres of grassland, with woods at intervals round its perimeter that serve as pheasant coverts. There are both fallow and red deer on the park, kept in place by miles of high iron railings, but at the first shot the deer always disappear to the other side of their enclosure, which incorporates all the grasslands but fences them out of the woodland. The deer were soon out of sight, that's how big the park is. The highland cattle and some rare breed sheep were less skittish; they just stared at us, unfazed by all the shooting.

Not far away from the police in the range rover was a gamekeeper from Sandringham with three Labradors sat close by, ready to pick up the game at his end of the line as soon as the ongoing 'drive' ended. He was wearing a tweed suit and tie – people say the Sandringham staff are more smartly turned out than the guns. Prince Philip had another Sandringham man to carry his gun and cartridges, but he also drove himself about, just like the Queen. The Royals love these shooting days, out of the sight of the public where they can really be themselves...

Anyway, the guns before us, arranged about forty yards apart, were each standing just behind their 'peg', which is a short stick with a card placed in the top. The cards are always numbered one to eight, from right to left. The ones I am describing were in a kind of horse-shoe shape around the end of the oblong-shaped wood. This means numbers 1 and

2, and 7 and 8 were placed at the sides to catch birds exiting to the left and right, with the middle numbers directly at the end of the wood where most birds tend to break out. The birds were driven towards us by a line of about fifteen beaters controlled by Helmingham's head gamekeeper. Most of the flushed pheasants soared up over the guns and reached a maximum height of about a hundred feet, just above the topmost twigs of the oak trees of the woods – not especially difficult targets for experienced guns. A few swooped low and were not shot at because they are considered too easy.

The expert shooters of the party brought down a great number with their double-barrelled 'side-by-side' shotguns, so that the parkland soon became littered with dead and dying birds, probably about fifty or sixty. Most were killed outright, but several fell wounded, so that between us and the guns were a large number of crippled birds, stumbling around with broken legs and wings. A few were 'runners', the name given to those brought down but still able to run. These are the first ones the dog handlers send their labradors and spaniels after, and often you can see a chase, as a dog courses after a flightless running pheasant. Occasionally, a bird hit in the wingtips slanted downwards and landed right behind us in the belt of trees that stood between us and the small country road that stretches between Helmingham Hall and the village of Framsden. The wounded birds there would be gathered later by hunting the strip of woodlands from end to end in a 'sweep' by two or more of the dog handlers. Thus, every effort is made to gather all the injured birds.

On the morning I am describing, right in the middle of the drive, there was suddenly a different kind of a 'flap', a little crisis brought on by a member of the paparazzi, armed with a long-lensed camera, straying onto the parkland by walking through the belt of trees behind us. Immediately the two royal protection squad officers from the far end of the line leaped into their range rover and set off after him. The officer from the Queen's land rover moved between her and the photographer, thus shielding her from both photographs and, if the man should be a terrorist in disguise, a bullet. That officer was taking no chances, though the Queen, after a quick glance behind her at the intruder, took no further notice of the little drama that was about to unfold.

While she watched her front to mark where the birds fell, the two policemen drove straight at the paparazzo and screeched to a halt right next to him. One officer covered him with a pistol, while the other grabbed him and threw him against the side of the vehicle. Then the officers frisked him, and took away his cameras. He looked absolutely petrified, as one of the officers, after opening his camera and confiscating the film, or maybe the card thing the modern ones use, marched him to a nearby gate, back through the trees, and ejected him onto the country road. There, I was later told, a waiting car with another paparazzo picked up the trespasser and whisked him away.

Later, we saw other cars on the country roads carrying people with cameras round their necks. Some of them were professional photographers trying to get a distant picture of the Royals, and others were just members of the public waiting for a glimpse of them as they sped past on their way to another 'drive' in a different part of the estate.

As for the police royal protection officers, I have a healthy respect for them – they're all pretty good at their job. I'd met them that morning at 8:30 a.m. on the Helmingham Estate main gate. Being a dog handler, I always went to the hall like the Royals, but instead of going in the front gate over the draw-bridge, I went to the kitchen for a coffee, which is on the north side of the sixteenth century building. When I'd arrived at the big gates leading to the main driveway there'd been two plainclothes officers on duty. One of them raised his hand and I'd pulled up alongside him and I wound down the window.

'Yes sir and who are you?' asked the first policemen very politely.

'I'm here with my dogs to pick up on the shoot,' I said. 'I'm Bob Benson.'

'Oh yes,' said the policeman, looking on his clipboard, 'I've seen you here before.'

'On you go, sir,' said the other policeman.

I drove a quarter mile down the private road and when I reached the moated hall I didn't pass over the drawbridge, but instead went around the back for my coffee. There were a half-dozen other cars parked in the stable yard, near to the back door leading to the kitchen. Labradors, spaniels and golden retrievers were milling around. Every time a dog crapped on the grass or gravel a little man with a bucket and shovel ran over and cleaned it up. I understand he was a gardener, and that was one of his less glamorous jobs.

Less than an hour later we all set off on the first drive

to pick up birds along with Her Majesty. Have you ever wondered what the Queen talks about when she makes small talk? Well, I'll tell you.

'Oh hello Mr. Benson,' she said as we got out of our vehicles, 'and how are you today?'

'Very well, ma'am,' I said; 'Nice morning for a shoot.'

'Yes,' she said smiling, 'No bright sun, no strong winds, no driving rain, no excuses!'

At this, the Duke of Edinburgh let out a little laugh.

'And who have you brought today?' she asked, pointing towards my two black labradors. 'That big boy, I think that's old Hunter isn't it?'

'Yes, ma'am,' I said; 'And the other one's Polly, his daughter.'

Because I'd been a regular at Helmingham for years and years the Queen knew my name, and my dogs' names. Actually, she always took a great interest in other people's dogs, but, truth be told, not so much in the dog handlers themselves.

A year earlier the Queen had instructed her dog handler and trainer, a Scotsman by the name of Bill Meldrum, to call me on the phone with some startling information.

'The Queen wants to buy your gundog Polly,' he said.

'Oh,' I replied.

'I can offer ye a good price, you canna say no; she'll be having an excellent life and she'll be running for Her Majesty the Queen.'

'I'm really sorry,' I said, 'but I'm afraid I can't sell.'

'No, man, you don't understand,' said Meldrum; 'The

Queen wants to buy your dog, and if it's the Queen that wants it, I canna tell her no!'

'But I can't sell, I'm really sorry,' I told him; 'You see that dog belongs to my wife, and she made me promise that I would never sell it. She means to have some pups from it, you see.'

'Aha, I understand,' said Meldrum, sounding rather worried; 'But how the hell am I gonna tell the Queen?'

'I'm sorry,' I said.

'Ah well,' said Meldrum, 'Never mind, I'm sure she'll understand...'

Well, if the Queen was a little miffed at not being able to acquire Polly she didn't show it. After the next drive, which was further along the park's perimeter, she spoke to me again:

'Mr Benson,' she said, 'You're a gamekeeper, perhaps you can suggest a way to solve a little problem we're having at the palace gardens. You see, the Canada geese are such a nuisance, they're fouling the lawn in the early morning before the gardeners arrive to shoo them off, and we don't know what to do.'

'Well, ma'am,' I said, 'Short of shooting them, the only thing to do is catch them up in cage traps, take them far away and clip their wings. That way they can't fly back again.'

'Yes, that's a very good idea,' she said; 'I don't know why somebody hasn't thought of that. But then we don't have a gamekeeper at the palace.'

Later on, at the mid morning 'elevenses' break, when I hovered a little way away from the party of guns, the Queen piped up to the steward who was dispensing sloe gin and snacks:

'Don't forget to give Mr. Benson some sausage rolls...'

And so, I got the same fare the Royals got, and even a shot of sloe gin in a plastic beaker. I felt a little awkward, as nobody else spoke to me, and none of the other dog handlers or servants, nor the policemen, were summoned closer, nor offered any refreshments...

Later we left the parkland and drove to a different part of the estate. We stood in the bottom of a valley for a partridge drive over open fields. There were a lot of birds driven over a thick hawthorn hedge, and as the guns were positioned here in a long straight line, it was possible for me to see all the guns in action in one place. I remember watching the Duke of Edinburgh in front of me. He was always like a dog off the leash on shooting days. He shot and shot in the shot, not just the birds in front of him but often ones in front of his neighbours. You could see he was really enjoying himself.

In contrast, Prince Charles went at it a little half-hearted, waiting until the birds had almost passed over his head and then missing. But Prince Andrew took after his father when it came to shooting. He took his birds early, right out in front, seldom missing, and when he did he sometimes swore.

Soon, that drive was reaching a crescendo. With flurry after flurry of partridges and a few pheasants rocketing over the guns, bird after bird was shot from the sky. An even greater number escaped over the guns, as they couldn't load in time, try as they might. Prince Andrew was fumbling in his cartridge bag, dropping ammunition into the mud. Prince Edward was in the thick of it, dropping pairs of partridges neatly with his left and right barrels. At one point, the Duke of Edinburgh had no birds in front of him, so he looked sideways, and seeing one approaching his oldest son, swung his barrels at it, fired, and dropped the partridge right at Prince Charles' feet. It was contrary to the rules of shooting etiquette, but the old boy didn't apologise, but only laughed at his little gaffe, before continuing to shoot birds coming directly at him.

At the end of the drive the head keeper blew his whistle and we saw the guns unloading their weapons, and their drivers pulled up ready to take them to the next covert. When they moved off, the Queen's land rover remained, with a detective left behind leaning on the bonnet. Meanwhile, the Queen sent her dogs scurrying across the field. A few seconds later, each had a partridge and was on its way back. Taking the partridges out of their mouths, she sent both dogs back to retrieve more birds.

I left all the birds in the open for the Queen, and concentrated on the birds that had fallen into the shelter belt further behind us. I and another handler sent our dogs into the thick cover, and picked the ones we'd see fall there.

Then we turned to watch the Queen working her dogs, but didn't send our own labradors. We were mindful of Lord T's instructions: 'When picking up at Helmingham, leave plenty of the easier birds for the Queen's dogs to find.' At one stage I remember she had a live partridge to despatch, which she did by expertly wringing its neck. When the last of the birds was gathered we met by the vehicles.

The Queen called out me saying:

'I think that's the last of them, Mr. Benson. Have you picked up those runners in the wood?'

'Runner' is the term used for a bird hit in the wing tips which angles down and then makes off on foot. Of course the Queen knows all the jargon – her family practically invented pheasant shooting.

'Yes ma'am,' I said. 'I think we're all clear here.'

I opened the back door of my land rover and my dogs jumped in. As they were still off the lead, the Queen's dogs also jumped in, our vehicles being similar models.

'Oh, I'm so sorry,' said the Queen; 'Come out of there you silly dogs.'

From what I saw, those dogs were the only ones allowed to disobey her. It was a funny world she lived in, where nobody contradicted or corrected her. Her conversation was sometimes a bit peculiar, like the discussions about the palace geese. But, to be fair, the other aristocrats are generally just as odd – they often seem to say the first thing that comes into their minds. We ordinary folk, on the other hand, are forbidden to initiate a conversation nor speak unless we're spoken to, and never, ever to look directly at them. And if you dared to take a photograph of any one of them on a shooting day... that would bring the detectives down on you, because showing the Royals out hunting is absolutely not allowed – everyone who attends the shoot knows that."

****

The fact that taking photographs was forbidden is rather telling. The ultra-loyal aides and courtiers who advise the Royal Family are keen to maintain the illusion of the Windsors being highly moral, squeaky-clean people who fulfil certain expectations the public have of them. It's a case of perception rather than reality. The Duke of Edinburgh, for instance, was Patron of the World Wildlife Fund, but still slaughtered thousands of game birds during his long life. The Queen was Patron of the Royal Society for the Prevention of Cruelty to Animals, and saw no irony or conflict of interests in the fact that she and her family routinely participated in blood sports. There is no suggestion here that she, or any member of her family broke any law while pursuing birds and animals – but I leave it up to the reader to decide for themselves the full implications of having a Royal Family that indulges in the violent 'sport' of game shooting.

CHAPTER TEN:
AN EXISTENTIAL THREAT – THE PATH OF AUSTRALIA AND OTHER COMMONWEALTH COUNTRIES

The Australian brand of Republicanism is like kryptonite for the British Royal family. The Australian republican movement has some interesting views on having a hereditary monarchy as their head of state. Some people in Britain are already looking at their model of government with interested eyes. Why? Because the Australian model has a blueprint for an elected head of state, effectively a president, to replace an hereditary monarch who has not been approved by an electoral vote.

The website of the 'Australian Republic Movement puts forward three basic premises:

1 <u>Australians should get a choice.</u>
Australians should have genuine merit-based choice about who speaks for then as Head of State, rather than a British King or Queen on the other side of the world.

2 <u>Australians should have a representative who has earned the position.</u>
To continue to allow such an important role to be handed down, from one generation of Royals to another is simply undemocratic. An independent country deserves to elect its own Head of State from a robust shortlist of Australia's most respected and trusted citizens nominated by Australia's parliaments.

3 <u>Australians should be represented by an Australian.</u>
It's time the Australian people chose one of our own to

represent us as our Head of State. Someone accountable to Australians, so that our future, more than ever, will be in Australian hands.

The Australians seem to have the election of a president figured out already. The 'Australian Choice Model' would allow every State and Territory Parliament to nominate one candidate for election to be Head of State. The Federal Parliament would be able to nominate up to three. Then they would hold a national election for Australians to decide which candidate should be Head of State.

Since 1901, the role of Head of State in Australia has been performed by the British King or Queen. Under the new system, Australia would be ruled by Australians instead. The Australian Choice Model would ensure the role of Head of State is ceremonial in nature, with limited powers to safeguard and maintain the constitutional order and resolve political gridlock. This is because Australian constitutional government already functions perfectly well without a president type figure with powers with, for example, like the USA's president.

Here is the OVERVIEW as they call it, of the Australian Head of State proposal:

Each State and Territory Parliament will be able to nominate one candidate for election. The Federal Parliament will be able to nominate up to three. Eligible nominees must be an Australian citizen, be eligible to be elected to the House of Representatives, not be a current sitting member of any Australian parliament and not have served more than one term as Head of State. A national election will be held to elect one of the nominees for a five-year term. We propose the same voting method that is used for House of Representatives elections be used for the election of the Head of State. If only one candidate is nominated (in total) by Australia's parliaments, voters will be empowered to confirm or reject that candidate at a national ballot.

A Head of State must act on the advice of the Prime Minister, Federal Executive Council or Ministers (as the case may be), except when: - Appointing the Prime Minister. They must determine who they believe is most likely to have the support in Parliament to form a Government, and are empowered to dismiss a Prime Minister who no longer has majority support (confidence).

The Model prohibits a Head of State from terminating the appointment of a Prime Minister who retains the confidence of the House. - Summoning Parliament to determine who has the confidence of the House of Representatives. - Calling an election where the confidence of the House remains indeterminate for more than seven days.

The Head of State would no longer be able to refuse to give approval (assent) or use their personal discretion to amend proposed laws that have passed the Parliament, or refuse to approve a constitutional change that has been approved by voters at a referendum. A Head of State may be removed by a motion passed in both Houses of the Parliament calling for their removal for proved misbehaviour or incapacity. In the event of the Head of State resigns, is removed or ceases to be eligible to hold office, the most senior State Governor serves as acting Head of State until such time as an election can be held. That the most senior

State Governor will also act as Head of State if the Head of State is absent or unavailable.

The role of 'Head of State' in Australia has been performed by the British king or queen. It's time for an Australian, chosen by Australians instead. The Australian choice model ensures the role of Head of State is ceremonial in nature, with limited powers to safeguard and maintain the constitutional order and resolve political gridlock.

This represents scary stuff for the Royal family. But all is not lost – yet. In an online Ipsos poll, conducted for the *The Age*, *The Sydney Morning Herald* and Nine News, only 34% of Australians said they wanted a republic in January 2021, while 40% said they'd prefer to keep the current system, and 26% didn't know. This was during the reign of the late Queen, and the effect of Charles' accession to the throne may have changed things significantly, as the following data shows...

In a Guardian Australia poll of 19 Sep 2022, Australians were asked whether they were 'pro' or 'anti' King Charles III. The survey took in 1,075 people, and was conducted shortly after Queen Elizabeth II's death. In the poll 43% of Australians supported Australia becoming a republic. 37% were now keen to keep the monarchy.

Ominously, the poll suggests there is less enthusiasm for the monarchy when questions relate specifically to King Charles III. When asked if King Charles III or Prince William should be Australia's head of state, voters were divided 50-50, with women, older voters and Coalition supporters more likely to back the older man as monarch. Thus, those doing the poll rated Prince William just as highly as his father.

Another question asked how positive Australians felt about various Royals. 44% gave the 73-year-old King a 'positive rating', whereas 63% felt positively about Prince William.

Interestingly, Prince Harry was more negatively rated than King Charles at 42% – with both viewed negatively by about 20% of voters.

Given that this is a small sample from only one region, it does nevertheless provide a significant insight into the way Australians are thinking. And, should Australians decide to break their ties with Britain by adopting a president type figurehead elected by a national vote, this could give a huge boost to the British Republic movement.

During, or just before the late Queen's reign, 29 Commonwealth countries became republics. As recently as 2021 Barbados opted to go the republican route and no longer have the British monarch as its nominal leader.

Canada is still largely in favour of having King Charles III as head of state. The monarchy costs them nothing, and the king is the only member of his family with a constitutional role. Thus, there is no question of them having to fund a large extended family. Members of the Royal family do visit from time to time in an official capacity, but they are treated merely as honoured guests rather than 'rulers'.

The real Head of State in Canada is the Governor General, a position appointed by the King, on the advice of his Canadian Prime Minister. The Governor General, in the king's name, performs most of his constitutional and ceremonial duties, and most Canadians are satisfied with this arrangement. The commission is for an indefinite period –

known as serving *at His Majesty's pleasure,* though five years is the usual length of time. Since 1959, it has also been traditional to alternate between Francophone and Anglophone office-holders – although many recent Governors General have been bilingual. By these means, Canadians are apparently at ease with the form of parliamentary democracy that governs that vast country.

A motion in November 2022 to sever ties with the monarchy put forward by the Bloc Quebecois Party, was defeated with 44 votes in favour to 266 against in the Canadian House of Commons. Bloc leader Yves-Francois Blanchet introduced the motion, saying allegiance to a foreign sovereign was not only outdated, but also expensive. 'The recent changing of the guard in England is an opportunity for Quebecers and Canadians to free themselves from a dilapidated monarchical link,' he stated before the motion was voted down.

Cutting ties with the monarchy would require Canada to amend its constitution with the support of all 10 provincial legislatures, as well as both houses of parliament. Quebec has never formally approved the constitution and many of its residents feel little attachment to Britain, polls show.

A growing number of Canadians also do not want a foreign monarch to represent them despite deep historical ties to Britain and affection for the monarchy, but there is little political will for constitutional reform. Their republican movement is strongest in Quebec where latest polls show 87% of citizens would prefer a true republic with a president, but elsewhere only 27% have a preference for abandoning a constitution headed by King Charles. It would appear that a stable system with a king that *costs them nothing*, appeals to the Canadian political conscience. Furthermore, Canadians are distanced from the negative aspects of having a royal family, such as wayward members of the clan attracting adverse publicity, as in the case of Prince Andrew. All things considered, it is difficult to see the constitution of Canada changing anytime soon.

The Commonwealth could be seen as a major reason the British should keep their monarchical system, since for the past 100 years the monarchy has been both a figurehead and unifying factor in this loose association of 54 countries and territories.

First established in 1887, the organisation allows each member to work towards shared goals of prosperity, democracy and peace. It was agreed in a conference in 1926 that they would all be equal members of a community within the British Empire, pledging allegiance to the King or Queen.

Of course, this does not mean that the United Kingdom actually rules over any participating Commonwealth countries, but only offers itself as a kind of master of ceremonies at international meetings, and puts forward proposals on which all countries vote on an equal basis. The list of Commonwealth countries is impressive: Antigua and Barbuda, Australia, Bahamas, Bangladesh, Barbados, Belize, Botswana, Brunei, Darussalam, Cameroon, Canada, Cyprus, Dominica, eSwatini, Fiji, Gambia, Ghana, Grenada, Guyana, India, Jamaica, Kenya, Kiribati, Lesotho, Malawi, Malaysia, Maldives, Malta, Mauritius, Mozambique, Namibia, Nauru, New Zealand, Nigeria, Pakistan, Papua New

Guinea, Rwanda, Saint Lucia, Samoa, Seychelles, Sierra Leone, Singapore, Solomon Islands, South Africa, Sri Lanka, St Kitts and Nevis, St Vincent and The Grenadines, Tanzania, Tonga, Trinidad and Tobago, Tuvalu, Uganda, United Kingdom and Vanuatu.

And King Charles III is actually head of state for Antigua and Bermuda, Australia, The Bahamas, Belize, Canada, Grenada, Jamaica, New Zealand, Papua New Guinea, Saints Kitts and Nevis, Saint Lucia, Saint Vincent and the Grenadines, Solomon Islands and Tuvalu.

The late Queen attempted to visit every country in the Commonwealth and make repeat visits. Charles will no doubt be visiting some of these. It is likely Prince William and the Duchess of Cambridge will undertake trips abroad to Commonwealth countries too. The King keeps in touch with Commonwealth developments through regular contact with the Commonwealth Secretary General and her Secretariat.

This is the Commonwealth's central organisation. Based in London, it co-ordinates many Commonwealth activities. His Majesty will also have regular meetings with Heads of Government from Commonwealth countries.

Whatever one's views on the role of monarchy, there can be little doubt that over the years the office of sovereign has played a huge part in international relations between Britain and the 54 Commonwealth countries. Defense, trade and environmental protection are important areas of cooperation that have developed over recent years. If Britain adopts a presidential style of leadership, the new head of state would need to take on all the duties associated with leading the Commonwealth.

Clearly, the new style of leader would have to know, or learn, a great many things about Britain's role in order to carry out his or her duties successfully.

CHAPTER ELEVEN:
THE MAGNIFICENT SEVEN – WHAT THEY WILL DO NEXT

As already stated, the new, slimmed-down firm will consist of King Charles III and Queen Consort Camilla, Prince Edward and Sophie, Countess of Wessex; The Duke and Duchess of Cambridge; and Anne, Princess Royal.

While all these individuals will be in the future representing the crown, Charles will take centre stage for important national events, such as the opening of Parliament, diplomatically receiving leaders of overseas countries, and the holding of royal ceremonies, such as his own coronation. It is likely he will work hard to try to impress upon the British people that he, Camilla, and the Cambridge family are making an excellent job of serving their country.

Charles' slimming down of the roles of his family could emulate the steps taken by Sweden's King, Carl Gustaf, who in 2019 stripped almost all of his grandchildren of their royal titles, with the exception of the future 'heir and spare' to the throne. Only the king of Sweden's eldest child Crown Princess Victoria and her two children will grow up to be working members of the royal family with titles. Cousins will have to get jobs outside of the monarchy.

In Britain a decree written in 1917 by George V states that only the children and great-grandchildren on the direct male line of the British monarch will gain official royal titles. Prince Harry's offspring Archie and Lilibet might have received titles now that the King has taken the throne. However, Charles is predicted not to grant these titles in keeping with the 'slimmed down' version of the monarchy he has in mind, and to thwart Harry and Meghan's using their 'royalness' for commercial reasons, such as to boost sales of their books and command higher fees for television appearances. Charles is said to be mightily upset by Harry's perceived disloyalty which has seen him make a lot of money out of revealing royal secrets and inside information.

Meanwhile, HRH Charles gets on with his plans for a revamp in London and the UK. A Palace insider said that, given you need a monarch in Buckingham Palace, Charles will put his royal advisors and office there, maintain apartments for a few sleepovers, and vacate the place whenever the opportunity affords it. Charles will not move into Buckingham Palace at all before the renovations underway are completed. Until then, the Palace will still be an entertaining venue, and will also still be open to visitors. The King has chosen to be based mainly at Highgrove until the Duchy of Cornwall and all its assets are fully turned over to William and Kate.

The Duke of Cornwall title has already gone to William, in accordance with the tradition that the eldest son of the sovereign will inherit the title. His Prince of Wales title has also been passed on, though no investiture ceremony is planned. There was even some speculation that Charles would give his Prince of Wales title to his brother, Prince Edward. Edward was, in fact, given the 'Duke of Edinburgh' title, previously held by his father.

Charles has something of a political dilemma at present, as he continues to champion issues he has long been passionate about, such as climate change. But as monarch, his options are a little more limited – for instance, Charles was advised not to attend the climate conference in Egypt in late 2022, much to his own frustration. But do not be surprised if Charles does, in future, take a more active stance in championing ecological matters – it is said he believes it is not beyond the scope of a king to participate in such matters.

Camilla, The Queen Consort, will have a prominent role in the new-look monarchy beside Charles. The 74-year-old became Queen Consort when Charles became King, as was the declared wish of the late Queen. She is a royal patron to several dozen charities and good causes, and will continue to accompany her husband on royal tours. Every year she meets thousands of people, and has gradually repaired her reputation following decades of criticism levelled at her for rekindling her relationship with Charles while he was still married to Princess Diana.

William and Kate, Duke and Duchess of Cambridge, will eventually occupy a part of Windsor Castle for some parts of the year. They have, as already stated, gained the extra titles of Duke and Duchess of Cornwall. William, as heir apparent will also inherit the title of Duke of Rothesay from his father. Thus, Kate will become known as the Duchess of Cambridge, Cornwall and Rothesay.

Some reports also suggest William and Kate could live in Clarence House when in London, which is due to be vacated by Charles. However, given their recent move to Windsor in order to be out of the constant gaze of the public and press, this seems unlikely at present. They are now living at Adelaide Cottage, a 10-minute walk from Windsor

Castle. Their three children, George, Charlotte and Louis, attend nearby Lambrook School, a private co-educational school in nearby Berkshire. The couple also maintain Anmer Hall on the Sandringham estate in Norfolk, given to them by the Queen, as their country bolthole. They are certainly not short of options when it comes to deciding where to live.

As regards their work engagements, on November 30 2022, William and Kate flew out to Boston, USA for a ceremony to name the five category winners of the Earthshot Prize. The possible winners included an electric vehicle manufacturer in Kenya, a recycling project in Amsterdam, and a desert agricultural system from China. Such an environmentally conscious competition is bound to resonate with the youth of Great Britain, but surely the elephant in the room is the fact that William and Catherine are themselves producers of an enormous carbon footprint – the Royal Family maintains at least 22 palaces, halls and grand residences. Their own share of these include Windsor, Anmer Hall in Norfolk plus usage of Balmoral, Sandringham and Kensington Palace. If William and Kate really want to find credibility amongst the young, environmentally conscious youth of Great Britain – and the world – they may have to change their lifestyle to practice what they preach. There is no point King Charles slimming down the monarchy to impress the British people if the working Royals are living overly lavish lifestyles which patently squander huge shares of the world's dwindling resources.

Perhaps they should follow the example of Princess Anne, The Princess Royal, second child of the Queen and, as stated earlier, the no-nonsense Royal with a somewhat inscrutable reputation. She lives with her family in a single property, Gatcombe Park in Gloucestershire. She will have an important role in Charles' slimmed-down monarchy. The first British royal to compete at the Olympics, in 1976, She has always had a good relationship with Charles, and it is difficult to see how her enormous workload could be passed on to other working members were she to dispose of her roles. The Princess Royal is currently patron to more than 300 different organizations and performs several royal duties each day. Unlike William and Kate, she will not be acquiring any new titles, but will remain as the Princess Royal, a title granted for life by Queen Elizabeth. She has said that she has no plans ever to retire from public service.

Likewise, Prince Edward, the youngest child of the Queen, and his wife Sophie will continue their royal duties. They have developed an ever more important role in recent years, following recent royal scandals with other family members. With Prince Andrew sidelined and removed as a key working royal, and Harry causing consternation with his steady release of damaging information about the Royal Family, Edward and Sophie are seen as steady, reliable supporters of Charles and the status quo. Residing at Bagshot Park in Surrey, the couple have taken on a significant increase in work following the departure of Harry and Meghan from royal duties. The Earl and Countess of Wessex were more prominent than almost any other member of the Royal family in the days leading up to Prince Philip's funeral in 2021, and have over *five hundred* royal patronages and duties to perform between them.

Prince Edward inherited the title of Duke of

Edinburgh from his father. Dickie Arbiter, a former royal press secretary said that this was his father's and mother's wish, and Charles was obliged to go along with this request.

Prince Andrew Prince Andrew was, as already outlined, sacked from frontline duties in November 2019 following his disastrous Newsnight interview about his relationship to Jeffrey Epstein and victim Virginia Roberts. It was then announced in January 2021 that the Prince would lose his royal patronages so that he could fight the allegations as a 'private citizen'. Despite repeatedly protesting his innocence, Andrew agreed to pay £12 million to settle the case before it reached a jury, and make a 'substantial donation' to her charity supporting victims' rights. By so doing, he has been judged by the world as guilty of Virginia Giuffre's allegations and treated by everyone accordingly. There will be no place for him in the new-look Royal Family.

Evidently, Andrew did try very hard to be rehabilitated with the Royal Family. There was surprise in March 2021 when Andrew was given a frontline role at the memorial service for the Duke of Edinburgh at Westminster Abbey. After arriving with the Queen, he assisted her as she walked to get to her seat. He also helped her out of the church and into the royal limousine at the end of the service. Prince William and Charles were opposed to allowing Andrew to escort the 96-year-old monarch to her seat in full view of the cameras and public, but their protests were overruled by the Queen, who made it clear she wanted her second son to have that prominent role.

However, surprisingly, Andrew was then banned

from appearing on the Buckingham Palace balcony for Her Majesty's Platinum Jubilee celebrations. On this occasion, William and Charles' strong demands were heeded by Her Majesty, a situation that royal experts interpreted as proving there was no path back for Prince Andrew. A very diplomatic palace spokesman said that the Queen had made the decision to restrict places on the balcony to 'working royals'. Later, Andrew had been set to attend the Service of Thanksgiving at St Paul's Cathedral but he then, rather conveniently, pulled out after testing positive for covid. Nor did he attend the annual Order of the Garter service at St George's Chapel in Windsor, though he had previously been listed on the order of service. Once again, it was said that Charles and Prince William demanded of the Queen that Andrew was sidelined from his former role – and sidelined, unfortunately for him, is where he is likely to remain for a long, long time...

CHAPTER TWELVE:
HARRY AND MEGHAN: BRITISH EXILE – OR AMERICAN FREEDOM?

On the subject of being sidelined, Prince Harry and Meghan will continue to stay out of frontline royal duties, having signalled their intention to stay in the US. They quit as senior members of the royal family in January 2020, when an agreement was announced that the couple would 'no longer be working members of Britain's Royal Family' and would lose their HRH titles.

After the couple moved to Montecito, California, Charles agreed to help support the couple from his private funds. But by March 2021 the couple's 'amiable split' from the firm had turned into an acrimonious feud, culminating in a shocking interview with US chat show host Oprah Winfrey, in which the pair laid bare some of the workings of the institution of monarchy which, they said, had conspired against them. They claimed they had been bullied and victimised by certain elements within the Palace's advisory team, and sparked a royal race row by claiming a senior royal had questioned the skin colour of their unborn first child. Both Harry and Meghan said they felt unsupported as members of the Royal Family.

But even after this Charles was still said to in regular contact with his son. A Palace source said that Prince Harry and Meghan remain 'much loved members of the family' but that it was hard for members of the family to get along with each other when intimate details were made public on international television. The Sussex's children Archie, and his sister Lilibet - seventh and eighth in line to the British throne – were said to be sources of sadness for the late Queen, since they lived in the USA. Charles is also, reportedly, full of regret for not having had the chance to spend more time with his grandchildren.

Tension was evident when Harry and Meghan visited the UK during the Queen's Platinum Jubilee celebrations in June, 2022. It was the first time that Her Majesty had met Harry and Meghan's daughter Lilibet, and the first time she had seen Archie in more than two years. But Her Majesty's decision to restrict the Buckingham Palace balcony appearances during Trooping the Colour and later in the Jubilee weekend to working royals meant that the Sussex's were excluded, and the public could only see Harry and Meghan as they travelled to and from the Palace.

Harry and Meghan did attend the Service of Thanksgiving at St Paul's Cathedral, their only official engagement of the entire weekend. The couple sat away from senior royals, in keeping with their new 'low' status within Clan Windsor. Harry and Meghan were then not seen again in public, but did meet the Queen at Windsor. The couple flew back to the US before the Jubilee celebrations ended. They returned to Britain for the 'One Young World' summit in Manchester on 5th September 2022, before flying to Dusseldorf to take part in an Invictus Games event, just before the Queen died.

At the funeral of HM The Queen on 19th September 2022 Harry and Meghan did actually sit with the senior Royals by the foot of the High Altar. Harry and Meghan were seated directly behind King Charles III and Queen Camilla, alongside their royal cousins, Princesses Beatrice and Eugenie, and Prince Edward and Sophie, Countess of Wessex. This was in keeping with the affection the Queen always had for Harry, despite his self-imposed exile away from the Royal Family. But Harry and Meghan's muted role before and after the funeral showed how far they were now removed from the British public. While Charles, Camilla, William and Kate met and thanked mourners, the Sussex's were sidelined into keeping a low profile, only being seen fleetingly in and around London and Windsor. They departed for the USA a few days later, an event almost unmarked by the British Press.

The next milestone in the Royal Family's rift with Harry and Meghan was airing of the three Netflix programs in late 2022. Then the launch of Harry's autobiographical book 'Spare' stirred up even more controversy. The book's title has a double meaning: as second son to Charles and Diana, Harry was the 'spare'child in case anything happened to Prince William. But in colloquial English 'spare' means angry, furious or mad with rage. The Royal Family had waited with trepidation to see what further intimate details the Prince would divulge to the world. Their nervousness was not allayed when the autobiography finally came out. Harry laid bare his resentment towards his stepmother Camilla. Harry wrote that Camilla had 'played a role' in his mother's death because she had been the reason that his parents' marriage failed. He did, however, concede that later he wanted his father and Camilla to be happy together. Harry was collaborating with the Pulitzer-winning ghostwriter J.R. Moehringer on what was described as 'the definitive account of the experiences, adventures, losses, and life lessons that have helped shape him'. One of these experiences involved being beaten up by his brother William. Another one involved having sex with an older woman in a field behind a pub. Yet another experience was his killing of 25 Taliban fighters while co-piloting an Apache helicopter in Afghanistan. There are other unflattering confessions too, but the book is at least a frank account of the first 38 years of Harry's somewhat bizarre and unconventional life.

So, what will Harry and Meghan do next? Not very much, it seems, other than spend some of the millions that their Netflix series and book royalties netted them. Ironically, under the new Charles III regime they could probably have found a way to remain in Britain. But now, as solely commercial entities, Harry and Meghan may be compelled to act out their role of victims many times over. The couple have professed a desire to be reconciled with King Charles, but, given the revealing content of their programs *and* the book, is this now likely?

The exiled couple certainly don't make things easy for themselves – in late 2022 Meghan invited controversial US comedian Trevor Noah on one of her podcasts. Noah has previously criticised, heavily and caustically, King Charles III for being a clueless, stressed-out king unsuited to high office – though Noah's suitability as a judge of kingship is open to debate. The point is, was Trevor Noah a wise or responsible choice of guest, considering the Sussex's supposed respect for Charles and the British monarchy? Did they also forget that their kudos as an exotic 'royal couple' is ultimately derived from respect for that same institution of monarchy? Accusations of their 'biting the hand that feeds them' have been raised, and there is some truth in the claim.

Meghan and Harry were rewarded at the 'Ripple of Hope Award' in 2022 for fighting injustice such as political or social oppression, including racism. And the reality is that the couple were nominated for *highlighting racism in the British royal family* in early December 2022

Piers Morgan in his 'Piers Morgan Uncensored' television channel angrily accused Harry and Meghan of being frauds. He lambasted the couple's eligibility for receiving the award. Guests on the show, however, applauded and supported the Duke and Duchess of Sussex for their stand, not just for pointing out racism, but also for other human rights issues. The Sussex's, it seems, even without being personally present, are box office dynamite, stirring debate and polarising factions wherever their standard is raised.

In this way, Harry and Meghan have continued the role Harry's mother Diana played, that of rebel-victim, fighting for justice and recognition that the stuffy and constricting courtiers of Buckingham Palace and Clarence House were unfairly maligning them for daring to try to live some kind of 'normal' family life.

But whereas Diana was usually loathe to fight or speak out against the Royal Family, Harry and his wife had no such qualms. By December of 2022 the slick publicity campaigns that were working to advertise their Netflix programmes and Harry's new book slipped into overdrive. The couple are big business in the USA and Britain, not to mention world-wide. In the first Netflix ad, Harry speaks the line: 'Nobody sees what's happening behind closed doors', which, when you give the sentiment two seconds of thought, is rather a silly thing to say. There are a series of still photos depicting the couple in idyllic poses, looking at each other lovingly. Then a picture of the massed paparazzi flashes onto the screen and Harry says: 'I had to do everything I could to protect my family.' The black and white photo shows a horde of photographers, with cameras sporting long lenses, looking at their quarry, which we assume are Harry and Meghan.

However, Sky News revealed that photograph came from the premiere of *Harry Potter and the Deathly Hallows: Part Two* way back in July 201. Oops! The cameramen were out to snap Daniel Radcliffe, Emma Watson Rupert Grint and the other members of the cast. This rather misleading use of the image conjures up the idea that the media went into a frenzy to photograph, perhaps even harass, the Duke and Duchess of Sussex. Furthermore, the trailer was released on the evening that the Earthshot prizes were being awarded in Boston, on 3rd December 2022. Thus, on Prince William and Kate's big night, Harry and Meghan also appeared in advertisements on all major TV channels, and featured on the evening news programs, overshadowing the Earthshot Prize.

In the second trailer, released on 5th December 2022, we see more sentimental shots of the Sussex's, before Harry says to camera 'Nobody knows the full truth. *We* know the full truth.' More still photos, and a voice says 'She's becoming a Royal rock star!' We see happy wedding shots and then the mood music and tone of the piece changes. A voice says: 'There was a war against Meghan to suit other people's agendas.' We then see images of a weeping Meghan. Harry says: 'There is a hierarchy of the family that is leaking but also planting the stories'. Pictures of Princess Diana make the link and suggestion that Meghan is being unfairly treated by the Royal Family. Meghan says in voiceover: 'I realised they were never going to protect me.' Pictures follow of her crying, while Harry says 'I was terrified – I didn't want history to repeat itself', i.e. for the Palace and media to hound Meghan to death as had happened to Princess Diana. The subject of race is again brought up, and Harry says: 'It's a dirty game.' Finally, Meghan says, in true movie-trailer style: *'When the stakes are this high, doesn't it make more sense to hear our story from us?'*

In the first three episodes of the much-hyped miniseries we see a love story unfold between an American actress and a British Prince. The real enemy of the couple, it turns out, is the British press. Constant intrusion into their personal life is a feature of their existence, and Meghan in particular is stressed and overwhelmed by the intensity of the interest in every aspect of their lives, not least her lavish wedding celebrations. But soon the strains of her new life become too much for her, and when she turns to her Royal aides, and members of the Royal Family for help, she is either ignored or told she must endure the pressures that go with her new status. Within months she is depressed and thinking suicidal thoughts, much to Harry's chagrin and regret. He sees in Meghan's plight a reminder of the way his mother suffered at the hands of the paparazzi, and realises something must be done.

In episode three we are confronted with the way Meghan's portrayal in the press and on social media goes from extreme popularity and endless praise, to a sudden fall from grace. After Harry and Meghan tour Australia, and are lauded both there and in Britain, there is a strong suggestion in the film that certain Royals in England – namely Prince William and Kate – are actually jealous of the Sussex's. Back in England, the press are mysteriously fed snippets of information detrimental to Meghan. The tone of the newspaper articles turns from adoration to criticism, with some barely disguised racism and misogyny.

Headlines appear such as 'Monster Markle Rips Royals Apart'. Another one read: '"Meghan's seed will taint our Royal Family" UKIP chief's glamour model lover, 25, is suspended from the party over racist texts about Prince Harry's wife-to-be.' Granted, this horrible piece of writing is quoting what a racist said, but was there really any need to highlight it as a headline, thus amplifying the bigot's reach a thousand-fold?

And when Meghan went to support the Grenfell Tower fire survivors by cooking a meal with Muslim women in a mosque, she was accused of supporting terrorists by more than one newspaper – simply because some male terror suspects had once attended the mosque years previously. Once again, there seems to be a smear campaign linking Meghan with unseemly people or events.

As already stated, Prince Harry appears to suggest in the film that Prince William and Kate's press office were giving the press negative stories about Meghan. One of these is that Meghan bullied members of her staff, and also reduced the Duchess of Cambridge to tears during a discussion over the Sussex's wedding plans. Furthermore, several papers and online news outlets suggested Meghan was being unfair and mean to her own father.

After their marriage, things got steadily worse. By the time their baby Archie was born, Meghan was distressed and bewildered by the once-adoring press giving out stories detrimental to her image. According to sources in the press, the newspapers never forgave Harry and Meghan for failing to present their baby on the steps of the hospital in which he was born. This, allegedly, broke the unspoken contract between Royals and the press whereby photo opportunities are supposedly given on such occasions. Harry said they had made a conscious decision not to parade their son, as was their right.

Only four months after Archie was born, Harry and Meghan toured South Africa, with the baby. Meghan was a big hit with the citizens of that country, but back in Britain many of the newspapers continued their barrage of articles casting Meghan – and sometimes Harry – in a bad light. Meghan's relationship with her father worsened when a letter to him was leaked to the press. The Sussex's sued The Mail on Sunday, thus making their relationship with the press even worse.

When the Sussex's decamped to Vancouver Island, Canada, for temporary respite from the press, journalists and members of the paparazzi soon learned of their whereabouts and harassed them there. Harry's proposal to his father and senior Royals that he wished to step back from full participation in the Royal Family while living abroad was, he says, mysteriously leaked to the newspapers. Harry considered this a breach of trust, perhaps perpetrated by Charles' press office. Back in England, on 20th January 2020 Harry was summoned to Sandringham House by Charles, the Queen and Prince William. Harry said that his plan to live abroad and still perform some royal duties was not even considered.

Harry maintains that he was frightened by William screaming and shouting at him, and that he was roundly told that either he was fully 'in' the Firm, or else must consider himself 'out'. Even before the meeting, the Daily Mail had branded Harry and Meghan 'The Rogue Royals' on 9th January. On the 12th the Times had written that William said 'I've put my arm around my brother all our lives. I can't do it any more.' The implication, as many people saw it, was that Harry was the one who'd withdrawn from the relationship.

Meanwhile, in response to the likelihood of the Sussex's going abroad, The Sun coined the unfortunate headline 'Megxit'. Social media, by this time, was stirred into a frenzy of anti-Meghan activity. In support of Meghan, Netflix episode number 5 claims that only 83 Twitter accounts had generated 70% of the hostile posts. It omits to say that Facebook, WhatsUp and the other outlets also showed a spike in anti-Sussex traffic. Though there were still those who chose to offer messages of support, a tide of anti-Meghan sentiment was definitely sweeping the United Kingdom.

In March 2020 the couple moved their North American base from Canada to Los Angeles, into the mansion of Tyler Perry, a Hollywood director who had great sympathy for the Sussex's. Soon after they arrived, Harry says the Daily Mail posted their address on its website. Paparazzi cut the wire fencing to get into the grounds of Perry's house, helicopters full of photographers circled overhead. Meghan had a miscarriage shortly after arriving in Los Angeles. Harry said in the film: 'I believe my wife suffered a miscarriage because of what The Mail did.' He later added: 'From what I saw, that miscarriage was created by what they were trying to do to her.' Having both suffered from mental health issues, Meghan and Harry engaged in 'Project Fearless' and other organisations helping mental health.

In one Netflix episode, Harry pointed to 'institutional gaslighting' by the aides of the Royal Family in England. He said: 'If you apply truth to power, that's how they respond'. He is thus inferring that by bravely confronting the Buckingham Palace aides, he and Meghan were unduly pressured and badly treated by Charles' and William's representatives.

Next, a clip of film shows a journalist confronting Prince William with the question 'Is the Royal Family a racist family?' This stops William in his tracks, and he responds: 'the Royal Family is very much *not* a racist family'. This part of the film was reportedly received very badly by William and Kate, and no wonder: the implication is that there was racism afoot in the Royal Family. As for the forced denial... was it *really* necessary to include that in a film about Harry and Meghan?

The last part of the Netflix film is devoted to the legal action that Meghan brought against The Mail On Sunday. Initially, she won her case, claiming that the letter she sent to her father being published amounted to breach of privacy; but The Mail On Sunday appealed. It brought in evidence from Jason Knauf, a former communications secretary for the Sussex's, who testified that he'd help compose the letter. The implication of his evidence was that she'd written it *knowing* it might be leaked. He said Meghan told him 'Everything I have drafted is with the understanding that it could be leaked, so I have been meticulous in my word choice.' It is unclear why Knauf decided to tell The Mail On Sunday all this, though some papers stated he was one of the staff Meghan had 'bullied' until he gave in his notice.

Despite this evidence, the British court of appeal upheld the judgement that publishing the letter was indeed a breach of Meghan's privacy, since she was entitled to expect that her personal correspondence to a family member remained private. The Netflix film ends with a statement about this matter. Clearly, Meghan was incredibly stressed by the whole legal wrangle, and by the conflict that had persisted between her and her father, Thomas Markle. She and Harry maintain that this fractured family relationship was caused by the news media tempting or causing her father to divulge highly personal information about her.

Two other things became clear from the Netflix series. Firstly, Harry and Meghan have passed the point of no return as regards the British press. By nailing their colours to the mast, and saying they won't be cooperating with journalists, and blaming the press for many of their troubles, they have ensured they will be hunted down wherever they go, and their actions scrutinized for news that might be twisted into articles critical of them.

Secondly, whatever their wishes, they are not going to be welcomed back into the Royal family, not ever. Rightly or wrongly, they have allowed Netflix to use hyperbole and great emotional impact to get across their message that they have been mightily wronged, and that both victimisation and racism were key parts of their having to leave the Royal Family and, ultimately, England.

So, what are the implications of all this as regards the future of the Royal family? Have the suggestions of racism and unfair treatment of Meghan, Duchess of Sussex, had any effect on the popularity and standing of the royal Family in general, and Charles and William in particular? Undoubtedly yes: there are only so many times that the slur of racism be cast upon prominent figures before the tide of public opinion moves to the point of believing that suggestion.

Nor do Prince William and King Charles emerge from this Netflix series smelling of roses on the subjects of bullying and family loyalty. On the contrary, it seems plain that senior Royals are prepared to sacrifice one of their own to maintain the status quo with the mighty British press. Why? Because Charles and William both are firmly held by the short and curlies when it comes to placating the daily papers *in order to keep public opinion in their favour.*

The question also needs to be asked: did they need to come down so hard on Harry and Meghan just because they wanted to spend part of their time abroad? Also, why didn't William and Charles *support* their fellow Royals when they were faced with unfair press and social media onslaughts?

If Harry's view of the in-fighting between the various Royal press offices is correct, instead of working together, some members of the three offices (the Sussex's, The Cambridge's and that of Charles) actively went into a civil war, a period of infighting between the family. If this is so, how bizarre a thing it was for the three departments to be stampeded into a right royal bun-fight when the real enemies at their gates all the time were the paparazzi, and the press-media tyrants who hounded them for stories.

And how much truth was there in the suggestion of the film that William and Kate were somehow so jealous of Meghan and Harry's rising popularity that they might have turned the press against them by drip-feeding negative gossip? The gossip included allegations of the bullying of staff by Meghan – though she in turn alleges *she* was the one bullied. In this great soap-opera of conflicting allegations, in this melee of royal scrimmaging, how ironic that the media got what it really wanted, namely a series of 'big' and dramatic Royal stories.

Truly, it bodes very ill for the future of the Royal Family that all these things really took place. What does it really say about their characters? About their sense of family values, about their courage when faced with the paper tigers armed with notebooks, or cameras camped outside their doors? Surely they are not living so much in fear of bad publicity that they are prepared to do these stupid, senseless and hurtful things to each other... are they? If so, it is time the Royal Family held yet another meeting, and asked each other if all that pomp and circumstance is really worth fighting over. Certainly, Harry and Meghan don't seem to think so. From their retreat in Los Angeles, perhaps it all seems a waste of time, and energy. How bizarre and senseless it is to live out one's life in constant fear of being derided and reviled by a news media that, like hunters of the last dodos, is prepared to kill off the very quarry it so assiduously seeks.

It appears that the Sussex brand will continue to make its fame and fortune by constantly referring back to the great wrongs that Prince William and Kate, and King Charles have done to Meghan and Harry. Many of the events took place many years before, for example the Sandringham summit at which William is said to have shouted at Harry was three years prior to the film about it. And yet we are told of these great wrongs as if they happened yesterday. But, without harping back to their exodus, and repeating how they were victims of a Royal plot to strip them of their power and status as the most 'popular' couple, the Sussex's have little of interest to tell the viewers. The Kardashians have their glamour and domestic dramas, the Osbournes have their wealth and weirdness, and the Sussex's are famous for... what? Victimhood? That is a slender basis for launching a six part documentary about their lives. On the other hand, however, the very fact that the Sussex's have been depicted in the domestic bliss of their private homes, nurturing their two children, working on their pet projects such as mental health charities and other good works, has set them up as icons for the modern world to observe, study and admire – a notion not a million miles away from the concept of 'royal-worship' they took so much trouble to escape from in the United Kingdom.

Having complained bitterly about their lack of privacy, how every aspect of their lives was scrutinized by unscrupulous journalists and crazed photographers, the public has now been shown close-up images of the Sussex's children, their dogs, the interiors of their houses, the security fences around their gardens, the cars they drive, even the things that make them cry. We see them walking hand in hand, swimming, working, cooking and looking after their children together. Many times the camera depicts them embracing, kissing, cuddling and enjoying romantic moments – and one naturally sees in all this a great irony, that in Britain they supposedly shunned the media and hated its close attentions, and now in Canada and the USA the intimate details of their lives have been put on show for billions of people around the world to take in... and one simply asks the question, *why?*

The answer can only be the 100 million dollars that, according to Forbes magazine, the couple received from Netflix. By receiving this, the Sussex's have secured their financial independence. But due to all the pressures placed on them, Meghan sacrificed the close relationship she had with her father. And Harry's sharpened darts have pierced the flanks of the Royal Family so many times, that surely, there is no way back for him even to have any relationship with his father and brother. He is now, truly, a prince in self-imposed exile.

CHAPTER THIRTEEN: THE RISING THREAT OF BRITISH REPUBLICANS

The Royal infighting is in many ways playing into the hands of the republican movement that is sweeping the United Kingdom. But do the 'republicans' actually pose a real threat to the Royal Family? Who exactly are these newly vociferous radicals who propose that Britain dispense with more than a thousand years of kings ruling these islands?

The truth is, that the Republican Party of Great Britain & Northern Ireland has a long history. Its foundations were laid in 1923, at the Labour Party's annual conference, when two motions were proposed, supported by Ernest Thurtle and Emrys Hughes. The first was that 'The Royal Family is no longer a necessary party of the British constitution', and the second was that 'The hereditary principle in the British Constitution be abolished'. While the party did not adopt so radical a concept as Republicanism, the seeds were sown for the future of the movement.

In 1936, following the abdication of Edward VIII, MP James Maxton proposed a republican amendment clause to the Abdication Bill, which would have established a republic in Britain. Maxton argued that the monarchy had 'outlived its usefulness'. Five MPs voted to support the bill, including Alfred Salter. The bill was defeated by 403 votes.

In 1983 the 'Republic' pressure group was formed. It was not taken seriously by the political parties of the time – republicanism was seen as a subject fit only for extreme left-wing political newspapers and student debating societies. In

1991, radical Labour MP Tony Benn introduced the Commonwealth of Britain Bill, which proposed the transformation of the United Kingdom into a 'democratic, federal and secular Commonwealth of Britain', with an elected president. He advocated that the monarchy would be abolished and replaced by a republic with a written constitution. It was read in Parliament a number of times until his retirement at the 2001 election but never achieved a second reading.

In January 1997, ITV broadcast a televised debate entitled *Monarchy: The Nation Decides,* in which 2.5 million viewers voted on the question 'Do you want a monarch?' by telephone. Speaking for the republican viewpoint were Professor Stephen Haseler (the then chairman of Republic), agony aunt Claire Rayner, Paul Flynn Labour MP for Newport West and Andrew Neil, former editor of The Sunday Times. Those in favour of the monarchy included author Frederick Forsyth, Bernie Grant, Labour MP for Tottenham, and Jeffrey Archer, former deputy chairman of the Conservative Party. The debate was conducted in front of an audience of 3,000 at the National Exhibition Centre in Birmingham. The telephone poll result revealed that 66% of voters wanted a monarch, and 34% opposed. So, it was a victory for the royalists, but still, *more than one third* of Britons had voted for a republic.

In the 21st century MORI polls in 2003 showed support for retaining the monarchy steady at around 70% of people, but in 2005, at the time of the wedding of Prince Charles and Camilla Parker Bowles, support for the monarchy was reduced to 65% of people who would support keeping the monarchy if there were a referendum on the issue, with 22% saying they favoured a republic. In 2009 a poll, commissioned by the BBC, found that 76% of those asked wanted the monarchy to continue after the Queen, against 18% of people who said they would favour Britain abolishing the monarchy.

In February 2011, a YouGov poll put support for ending the monarchy after the Queen's death at only 13%, if Prince Charles became king. In April 2011, an Ipsos MORI poll of 1,000 British adults found that 75% of the public would like Britain to remain a monarchy, with 18% in favour of Britain becoming a republic.

In September 2015, Jeremy Corbyn, a Labour MP with republican views, won his party's leadership election and became both Leader of the Opposition and Leader of the Labour Party. In 1991, Corbyn had seconded the Commonwealth of Britain Bill. However, Corbyn made it clear he would no longer be advocating the Republican cause.

A group of MPs that included Richard Burgon, Laura Pidcock, Dennis Skinner and five others expressed sympathy for an oath to their constituents rather than to the monarch when being sworn into office.

In May 2021, a YouGov poll put support for the monarchy down at 61% among all over-18s, with a particularly high rise in republican views in the 18–24 age group (41%).

In May 2022 another YouGov poll showed that only 31% of 18–24 year olds were in favour of the monarchy, compared to 66% of the population as a whole.

But by January 6 2023, after Charles had been king for 3 months, things had changed markedly. 35% of those questioned by YouGov had an unfavourable view of the British monarchy. This figure is surprisingly high – most commentators had thought King Charles was proving quite popular in his new role. Another poll among students across three different campuses showed that only 41% favoured keeping Charles as king, with 47% opting for a republic. Is the tide beginning to turn against the House of Windsor? It would appear so, and would tie in with a surge in interest in the Republican Party of Great Britain & Northern Ireland.

Their website states the following aims:

The monarchy will be peacefully abolished and a parliamentary republic will be formed in its place.
The Head of State, the President, will be elected by the people on a four year term.
The President's role will be to uphold the constitution.
The Prime Minister and parliament will continue to govern the country, with the President's role being largely ceremonial.

The Republican Party gives voice to the significant proportion of British people who do not support the Monarchy. It is an understatement to say that the British people who felt this way were badly organised in the past. There seems to have been a common belief that resistance to the Royal Family's heading the constitution was futile and unpatriotic. During the late 20th century, and particularly in the past 20 years, a shift has occurred in thinking, fuelled by what is deemed unacceptable behaviour by some Royals, and a growing disgust at the conspicuous waste of money and resources enacted by the House of Windsor. The growth of the internet and social media resources has meant that once isolated voices are now combining and colluding to express ways in which Britain may be governed by an altogether more democratic system.

The Republican Party manifesto says:

> The Conservatives and Labour have ruled the UK for over one hundred years. It's time for change. We envisage a bright future for Britain; a future that's more democratic, more liberal, and full of opportunity to all citizens regardless of their status at birth.
>
> We will reform our broken electoral system by using proportional representation in all national and local elections.
>
> We will reform our political system by making our Head of State and upper house electable.
>
> We will protect free speech by bolstering free speech laws and punishing media and educational institutions that show disregard for freedom of expression.
>
> We will break up monopolies and crack down on crony capitalism so that the free market can function efficiently.
>
> We will protect people's personal beliefs by making the country more secular. Believers and non-believers alike will be free from government interference in their religion, or lack thereof.

So, how nervous should the Royal Family be, when confronted by an organised and growing political movement whose avowed intention is to replace them with a single elected presidential leader? Do they, in their heart of hearts, know that an autocratic, hereditary king or queen is the wrong option for Great Britain? Certainly, the aims of the Republicans seem reasonable enough. They advocate:

1. The Head of State should be elected.
2. The House of Lords should be abolished and replaced with an elected upper house.
3. Elections should use Proportional Representation.
4. An English Parliament should be established with powers similar to those of the Scottish Parliament.
5. Encouraging free enterprise is the key to creating wealth and funding public services.
6. All religious institutions should be separated from the state.

But there are two obstacles to such a radical program which may make their manifesto unobtainable. The first is the inherent resistance to political change that is typical of British society. The second is the fact that change to the House of Lords and monarchy itself will be staunchly resisted by many politicians across all parties. The Conservative Party in particular has a majority of MP's in the Commons that will not vote for reform, and the House of Lords has even more members who will not look favourably on abolishing the office of king or queen.

But there is one factor that may just make some form of change inevitable. That is the rising number of young people who are dissatisfied with the Royal Family's expense and hypocrisy at advocating environmental issues while themselves living extravagantly and consuming vast amounts of fossil fuels and resources. The fact that in the past so many members of the family were receiving direct or indirect payments through the Sovereign Grant system did not go down well with a broad swath of the general public. At a time of rising prices, with wages falling in real terms, and with things particularly difficult for disaffected young people, the granting of millions of pounds to the already well-off Windsor family has created criticism on social media platforms.

Movements to criticise and 'cancel' those who are deemed 'bad' or in some way sinning against modern values can be stirred up in a matter of hours. The fate of Lady Susan Hussey who asked a black British lady 'where she was really from' has sent shockwaves through the Royal Family. One minute Lady Susan, a former companion of the Queen was helping Queen Consort Camilla host a reception for a British charitable organisation, and the next she was being shouted down as a racist and bully who belittled those she perceived as being non-British because of their ethnicity. This demonstrates how establishment figures who give out signs that they have unacceptable views will be mercilessly pilloried by the public and the press. There is no road back, as Prince Andrew has already found out. One wonders just how many more instances there will be in the future before the public turns on them in a more serious and protracted way. These incidents which reveal the inner beliefs and attitudes of the Royal Family and their entourage are fuel for the fire of British republicanism. If a president or politician has unacceptable views or does something that offends, he or she may be removed. The problem with a prince or king is that he or she adopts a leadership role simply by being born into the right family – even if the person in question is a bumbling fool, a walking environmental disaster or a monstrous hypocrite. But, rest assured, no position is safe in today's 'cancel culture' society, not even that of king. It is not inconceivable that a monarch be so pressured by social media, the press, and the public protesting in the street that he either abdicates, or is asked to stand down by Parliament.

There is one final point to make about having a king as head of state, a person the country supposedly looks up to. The crux of the matter is why anyone should believe a single person is so special, somehow so intrinsically good that they deserve to be given our unlimited respect in the first place. In the past non-aristocratic folks might be bamboozled into worshipping and obeying their monarch, impressed by their stately bearing, their clothes, their air of superiority. But in today's society, with everybody having some level of education, access to information online, and a more questioning, egalitarian mindset, will the British people continue to be dazzled by the 'magic' of royalty? And can the institution of monarchy stand up to having its king and heir, not to mention his close relatives, scrutinized and examined under the microscope of public opinion?

With all the media attention now focused on the Royal family, with all the gossip and critical social media traffic poring over every small action the Royals make, it is by no means certain the younger generation in particular will buy into the mystery, magic, pomp and ceremony that is, by its very nature, a thing of the past, in the real sense of the word, an anachronism.

Change is coming, that much is certain. Royalty will need to evolve, adapt and learn how to do things professionally and with a minimum of fuss if it is to survive.

Until now, people have feared altering the political hierarchy in case the new system proves worse than the one we already have. But it may be only a matter of time before the winds of change grow strong enough to sweep away the old, in favour of a political structure more fitting for the United Kingdom and Commonwealth in the twenty-first century.

APPENDIX 1 – OPRAH'S INTERVIEW WITH PRINCE HARRY AND MEGHAN MARKLE SUNDAY 7TH MARCH 2021

All those interested in the British Royal Family should read this interview in full to decide for themselves whether Meghan and Harry are telling the truth – or perhaps have prepared a highly controversial narrative to persuade the TV audience that it is they who have been 'wronged' and should have the 'moral high ground'.

The British press have cast doubt on almost all of Meghan's statements, which include how senior members of the Royal Family asked questions about their unborn baby's likely skin colour, and how Princess Kate the Duchess of Wessex made Meghan cry. Meghan, however, puts forward a view that she was victimised and put down by Kate and senior Royals, and that the press turned against her when she refused to let her baby Archie be photographed shortly after his birth.

Furthermore, Meghan, Duchess of Sussex laments how, having fallen from royal favour, her British police bodyguards were suddenly withdrawn, and that the senior Royal Family members deliberately released bad publicity about her to the press. She also states that Harry was vindictively starved of money to maintain his family at a crucial time. There are other very serious allegations too – allegations which Meghan and Harry advocate as solid facts – that would, if true, mean that the senior Royals were responsible for driving Meghan almost to suicide.

The only way to really judge the veracity of Meghan

and Harry's claims is to read the following tape-script, and decide for yourself how much of it rings true, and how much of it might be the embittered narrative of a couple who believe they have been mightily wronged. Either way, it certainly makes a fascinating read and sheds a lot of light on the British Royal Family, and its own unique and very peculiar brand of family feuding.

THE INTERVIEW

Oprah: We can't hug, everybody is double- masked and has face shields. You look lovely. Do you know if you're having a boy or a girl?

Meghan: We do this time. I'll wait for my husband to join us and we can share that with you.

Oprah: That would be really great. Before we get into to it, I just want to make clear to everybody that, even though we're neighbours, I'm down the road, you're up the road, we're using a friend's place. There has not been an agreement, you don't know what I'm going to ask, there is no subject that's off limits and you are not getting paid for this interview.

Meghan: All of that's correct.

Oprah: I remember sitting in the chapel — thanks for inviting me, by the way. I so recall this sense of magic. I never experienced anything like it. When you came through that door, you seemed like you were floating down the aisle. Were you even inside your body at that time?

Meghan: I've thought about this a lot. It was like having an out-of- body experience I was very present for. The night before, I slept through the night entirely, which is a bit of a miracle, and then woke up and started listening to Going To The Chapel, to make it fun and light and remind ourselves this was our day. We were both aware in advance of that this wasn't our day, this was the day planned for the world.

Oprah: Everybody who gets married knows you're really marrying the family. But you weren't just marrying a family, you were marrying a 1,200-year-old institution, you're marrying the monarchy. What did you think it was going to be like?

Meghan: I would say I went into it naively because I didn't grow up knowing much about the Royal Family. It wasn't part of something that was part of conversation at home. It wasn't something that we followed. My mum even said to me a couple of months ago, 'Did Diana ever do an interview?' Now I can say. 'Yes, a very famous one', but my mum doesn't know that.

Oprah: But you were aware of the royals and, if you were going to marry into the royals, you'd do research about what that would mean?

Meghan: I didn't do any research about what that would mean.

Oprah: You didn't do any research?

Meghan: No. I didn't feel any need to, because everything I needed to know he was sharing with me. Everything we thought I needed to know, he was telling me.

Oprah: So, you didn't have a conversation with yourself, or talk to your friends about what it would be like to marry a prince, who is Harry, who you had fallen in love with – and you didn't give it a lot of thought?

Meghan: No. We thought a lot about what we thought it

might be. I didn't fully understand what the job was: What does it mean to be a working royal? What do you do? What does that mean? He and I were very aligned on our cause-driven work. That was part of our initial connection. But there was no way to understand what the day-to-day was going to be like, and it's so different because I didn't romanticise any element of it. But I think, as Americans especially, what you do know about the royals is what you read in fairytales, and you think is what you know about the royals. It's easy to have an image that is so far from reality, and that's what was so tricky over those past few years, when the perception and the reality are two different things and you're being judged on the perception but you're living the reality of it. There's a complete misalignment and there's no way to explain that to people.

Oprah: With every family things get serious when you're brought in to meet the grandmother or the mother. The grandmother is the matriarch and, in your situation it's the Queen.

Meghan: She was one of the first people I met. The real Queen.

Oprah: What was that like? Were you worried about making the right impression?

Meghan: There wasn't a huge formality the first time I met Her Majesty The Queen. We were going for lunch at Royal Lodge, which is where some other members of the family live, specifically Andrew and Fergie, and Eugenie and Beatrice would spend a lot of time there. Eugenie and I had known each other before I knew Harry, so that was comfortable and it turned out the Queen was finishing a

church service in Windsor and so she was going to be at the house. Harry and I were in the car and he says, 'OK, well my grandmother is there, you're going to meet her'. I said 'OK, great'. I loved my grandmother, I used to take care of my grandmother. He said 'Do you know how to curtsey?' 'What?' 'Do you know how to curtsey?' I thought genuinely that's what happens outside, that was part of the fanfare. I didn't think that's what happens inside. I go, 'But it's your grandmother'. He goes, 'It's the Queen!'
Oprah: Wow!
Meghan: And that was really the first moment the penny dropped?
Oprah: Did you Google how to curtsey?
Meghan: No, we were in the car. Deeply, to show respect, I learned it very quickly right in front of the house. We practised and walked in.
Oprah: Harry practised?
Meghan: Yeah, and Fergie ran out and said, 'Are you ready? Do you know how to curtsey? Oh, my goodness, you guys'. I practised very quickly and went in, and apparently, I did a very deep curtsey, and we just sat there and we chatted and it was lovely and easy and I think, thank God, I hadn't known a lot about the family. Thank God, I hadn't researched. I would have been so in my head about all of it.
Oprah: What you're sharing with us is that you were no more nervous as a regular person who goes to meet somebody's grandmother.
Meghan: I had confused the idea. I grew up in LA, you see celebrities all the time. This is not the same but it's very easy, especially as an American, to go, 'These are famous people'.

This is a completely different ball game.
Oprah: What are you feeling here? What's the word?
Meghan: Peace.
Oprah: Peace?
Meghan: Yeah.
(**Oprah** narrates) The day after our interview, I stopped over to Harry and Meghan's new home.
Meghan: Hi, Guy (dog).
Oprah: Hi, Guy.
Meghan: Yeah, Guy's been — Guy's been through everything with me.
Oprah: Yeah, from the beginning, from the very first date, yeah?
Meghan: If Guy, I mean, I had him in Canada. I got him from a kill shelter in Kentucky.
Oprah: Yeah?
Meghan: Hi, girls!
(**Oprah** narrates) We put on wellies to feed the hens Meghan and Harry recently rescued from a factory farm. 'I love your little designer house here. Archie's chick inn. Oh, how cute is that.'
Harry: She's always wanted chickens.
Meghan: Well, you know, I just love rescuing.
Oprah: So, this is a part of your new life? What are you most excited about?
Meghan: Whoop! You're OK...
Oprah: What are you most excited about in the new life? What are you most excited about? Here, chick, chick, chick, chick.
Meghan: I think just being able to live authentically.

Oprah: Mm-hmm.

Meghan: Right? Like this kind of stuff. It's so, it's so basic, but it's really fulfilling. Just getting back down to basics. I was thinking about it — even at our wedding, you know, three days before our wedding, we got married...

Oprah: Ah!

Meghan: No one knows that. But we called the Archbishop, and we just said, 'Look, this thing, this spectacle is for the world, but we want our union between us'. So, like, the vows that we have framed in our room are just the two of us in our backyard with the Archbishop of Canterbury, and that was the piece that...

Harry: Just the three of us.

Oprah: Really?

Harry: Just the three of us.

Meghan: Just the three of us.

Oprah: You know, the wedding was the most perfect picture, you know, anybody's ever seen. But through that picture that we were all seeing, behind the scenes, obviously, there was a lot of drama going on. And soon after your marriage, the tabloids started offering stories that painted a not-so-flattering picture of you in your new world. There were rumours about you being 'Hurricane Meghan'.

Meghan: I hadn't heard that.

Oprah: So, there were rumours about you being Hurricane Meghan, for the departure of several high-profile palace staff members. And there was also a story — did you hear this one — about you making Kate Middleton cry?

Meghan: This I heard about.

Oprah: You heard about that. OK.

Meghan: This was... that was... that was a turning point.
Oprah: That was a turning point?
Meghan: Yeah. Kate made me cry days before the wedding, but I got blamed... that was hard.

(Oprah narrates) Six months after Harry and Meghan's wedding, headlines began to swirl about a rift between Meghan and her sister-in-law, the Duchess of Cambridge, Kate Middleton. It was reported that Meghan had left Kate "in tears" over the bride-to-be's "strict demands" over flower-girl dresses.

Meghan: The narrative with Kate — which didn't happen — was really, really difficult and something that ... I think that's when everything changed, really.
Oprah: You say the narrative with Kate, it didn't happen. So, specifically, did you make Kate cry?
Meghan: No.
Oprah: So, where did that come from?
Meghan: (Sighs)
Oprah: Was there a situation where she might have cried? Or she could have cried?
Meghan: No, no. The reverse happened. And I don't say that to be disparaging to anyone, because it was a really hard week of the wedding. And she was upset about something, but she owned it, and she apologised. And she brought me flowers and a note, apologising. And she did what I would do if I knew that I hurt someone, right, to just take accountability for it. What was shocking was... what was that, six, seven months after our wedding?
Oprah: Mm-hmm.
Meghan: That the reverse of that would be out in the world.

Oprah: The story came out six, seven months after it actually happened?

Meghan: Yeah.

Oprah: So, when you say...

Meghan: I would have never wanted that to come out about her ever, even though it had happened. I protected that from ever being out in the world.

Oprah: So, when you say the reverse happened, explain to us what you mean by that.

Meghan: A few days before the wedding, she was upset about something pertaining — yes, the issue was correct — about flower-girl dresses, and it made me cry, and it really hurt my feelings. And I thought, in the context of everything else that was going on in those days leading to the wedding, that it didn't make sense to not be just doing whatever everyone else was doing, which was trying to be supportive, knowing what was going on with my dad and whatnot.

Oprah: This was a really big story at the time, that you made Kate cry. Now you're saying you didn't make Kate cry, Kate made you cry. So, we all want to know, what would make you cry? What... what were you going through? You were going through all of the anxiety that brides go through putting their wedding together and going through all of the issues with your father: Was he coming? Was he not coming? And there was a confrontation over the... the dresses?

Meghan: It wasn't a confrontation, and I actually don't think it's fair to her to get into the details of that, because she apologised.

Oprah: OK.

Meghan: And I've forgiven her.

Oprah: Mm-hmm.

Meghan: What was hard to get over was being blamed for something that not only I didn't do but that happened to me. And the people who were part of our wedding going to our comms team and saying, 'I know this didn't happen.' I don't have to tell them what actually happened.

Oprah: OK.

Meghan: But I can at least go on the record and say she didn't make her cry. And they were all told the same...

Oprah: So, all the time the stories were out that you had made Kate cry... you knew all along, and people around you knew that that wasn't true?

Meghan: Everyone in the institution knew it wasn't true.

Oprah: So, why didn't somebody just say that?

Meghan: That's a good question. I'm not sharing that piece about Kate in any way to be disparaging to her. I think it's really important for people to understand the truth.

Oprah: Mm-hmm.

Meghan: But also I think, a lot of it, that was fed into by the media. And I would hope that she would have wanted that corrected, and maybe in the same way that the Palace wouldn't let anybody else.

Oprah: Yeah.

Meghan: Negate it, they wouldn't let her, because she's a good person. And I think so much of what I have seen play out is this idea of polarity, where if you love me, you don't have to hate her. And if you love her, you don't need to hate me.

Oprah: Mm-hmm. You know, there were several stories that

compared headlines written about you to those written about Kate. Since you don't read things, let me tell you what was said.
Meghan: OK.
Oprah: There were stories where Kate was being praised for holding her baby bump.
Meghan: Oh, gosh, have I done it since we've been sitting down?
Oprah: Yes, you've been doing it the whole time.
Meghan: Probably. OK.
Oprah: Kate was praised for cradling her baby bump, and the headline about you doing the same thing said, 'Meghan can't keep hands off her baby bump for pride or vanity'.
Meghan: What does it have to do with pride or vanity?
Oprah: Well, I'm just — I'm just telling you about the stories, OK?
Meghan: OK, I hear you.
Oprah: Then there was a whole online piece about this: 'Kate eating avocados to help with morning sickness'.
Meghan: I heard — OK, I heard about the avocado one.
Oprah: But you were eating avocados...
Meghan: And fuelling murder, apparently.
Oprah: Wolfing down a fruit linked to water shortages, illegal deforestation and environmental devastation. There was, seems... there seems to be... there was a...
Meghan: That's a really loaded piece of toast. (Laughter) I mean... you have to laugh at a certain point, because it's just ridiculous.
Oprah: That's good: 'That's a loaded piece of toast.' It's about deforestation and...

Meghan: Oh, man!

Oprah: Oh, wow! So, do you think there was a standard for Kate in general and a separate one for you? And if so, why?

Meghan: I don't know why. I can see now what layers were at play.

Oprah: Mm-hmm.

Meghan: And, again, they really seemed to want a narrative of a hero and a villain.

Oprah: Yeah. You came in as the first mixed-race person to marry into the family, and did that concern you in being able to fit in? And did that concern you in being able to fit in? Did you think about that at all?

Meghan: I thought about it because they made me think about it.

Oprah: Mm-hmm.

Meghan: Right? But at the same time now, upon reflection, thank God all of those things were true. Thank God I had that life experience. Thank god I had known the value of working. My first job was when I was 13, at a frozen yoghurt shop called Humphrey Yogart.

Oprah: Mm-hmm.

Meghan: I've always worked. I've always valued independence. I've always been outspoken, especially about women's rights. I mean, that's the sad irony of the last four years... is I've advocated for so long for women to use their voice, and then I was silent.

Oprah: Were you silent? Or were you silenced?

Meghan: The latter.

Oprah: So, how does that work? Were you told by the comms people, or the, I don't know, the institution? Were you told to keep silent? How were you told to handle tabloids or gossip? Were you... were you told to say nothing?

Meghan: Everyone from... everyone in my world was given very clear directive, from the moment the world knew **Harry** and I were dating, to always say, 'No comment'. That's my friends, my mom and dad.

Oprah: Mm-hmm.

Meghan: And we did.

Oprah: Mm-hmm.

Meghan: I did anything they told me to do — of course I did, because it was also through the lens of, 'And we'll protect you'. So, even as things started to roll out in the media that I didn't see — but my friends would call me and say, 'Meg, this is really bad' — because I didn't see it, I'd go, 'Don't worry. I'm being protected'.

Oprah: Mmm.

Meghan: I believed that. And I think that was... that was really hard to reconcile because it was only... it was only once we were married and everything started to really worsen that I came to under-stand that not only was I not being protected, but they were willing to lie to protect other members of the family but they weren't willing to tell the truth to protect me and my husband.

Oprah: So, are you saying you did not feel supported by the powers that be, be that The Firm, the monarchy, all of them?

Meghan: It's hard for people to distinguish the two because there's... it's a family business, right?

Oprah: Mm-hmm.

Meghan: So, there's the family, and then there's the people

that are running the institution. Those are two separate things. And it's important to be able to compartmentalise that, because the Queen, for example, has always been wonderful to me. I mean, we had one of our first joint engagements together. She asked me to join her, and I . . .
Oprah: Was this on the train?
Meghan: Yeah, on the train.
Oprah: Yeah.
Meghan: We had breakfast together that morning, and she'd given me a beautiful gift, and I just really loved being in her company. And I remember we were in the car . . .
Oprah: Can you share what the gift was? Or . . .
Meghan: Yes. She gave me beautiful pearl earrings and a matching necklace. And we were in the car going between engagements, and she has a blanket that sits across her knees for warmth. And it was chilly, and she was like, 'Meghan, come on' and put it over my knees as well.
Oprah: Oh, nice.
Meghan: Right. Just moments of . . . and it made me think of my grand-mother, where she's always been warm and inviting and . . . and really welcoming.
Oprah: So, OK, so she made you feel welcomed?
Meghan: Yes.
Oprah: Did you feel welcomed by everyone? It seemed like you and Kate . . . at the Wimbledon game where you were going to watch a friend play tennis . . . Was it what it looked like? You are two sisters-in-law out there in the world, getting to know each other. Was she helping you, embracing you into the family, helping you adjust?
Meghan: I think everyone welcomed me.

Oprah: Mm-hmm.

Meghan: And, yeah, when you say, 'Was it what it looked like?', my understanding and my experience of the past four years is it's nothing like what it looks like. It's nothing like what it looks like. And I ... and I remember so often people within The Firm would say, 'Well, you can't do this because it'll look like that. You can't'. So, even, 'Can I go and have lunch with my friends?' 'No, no, no, you're oversaturated, you're every-where, it would be best for you to not go out to lunch with your friends'. I go, 'Well, I haven't ... I haven't left the house in months'. I mean, there was a day that one of the members of the family, she came over, and she said, 'Why don't you just lay low for a little while, because you are everywhere right now'. And I said, 'I've left the house twice in four months. I'm everywhere, but I am nowhere'. And from that standpoint, I continued to say to people, 'I know there's an obsession with how things look, but has anyone talked about how it feels? Because right now, I could not feel lonelier'.

Oprah: Hmm. You were feeling lonely, even though your prince ... you're in love, you're with him.

Meghan: I'm not lonely ... I wasn't lonely with him.

Oprah: Yeah.

Meghan: There were moments that he had to work or he had to go away, there's moments in the middle of the night. And so, there was very little that I was allowed to do.

Oprah: Mm-hmm.

Meghan: And so, yeah, of course that breeds loneliness when you've come from such a full life or when you've come from freedom. I think the easiest way that now people can

understand it is what we've all gone through in lockdown.
Oprah: Well, I would have to say, in South Africa, when the reporter stopped and asked, 'Are you OK . . ?'
Meghan: Mmm.
Oprah: And, whooo, we all felt that. Why did that question strike such a nerve? What was going on with you, internally at that time?
Meghan: That was the last day of the tour. You know, those tours are . . . I'm sure they have beautiful pictures and it looks vibrant, and all of that is true. It's also really exhausting. So, I was fried, and I think it just hit me so hard because we were making it look like every-thing was fine. I can understand why people were really surprised to see that there was pain there.
Oprah: Mm-hmm.
Meghan: Because we were doing our job. Our job was to be on and to smile. And so, when he asked me that, I guess I had felt that it had never occurred to anyone that I, that I wasn't OK, and that I had really been suffering. And I had known for a long time and had been asking the institution for help for quite a long time.
Oprah: Help for what?
Meghan: After we had gotten back from our Australia tour — which was about a year before that — and we talked about when things really started to turn, when I knew we weren't being protected. And it was during that part of my pregnancy, especially, that I started to understand what our continued reality was going to look like.
Oprah: What kind of protection did you want that you feel you didn't receive?

Meghan: I mean, they would go on the record and negate the most ridiculous story for anyone, right? I'm talking about things that are super-artificial and inconsequential. But the narrative about, you know, making Kate cry, I think was the beginning of a real character assassination. And they knew it wasn't true. And I thought, well, if they're not going to kill things like that, then what are we going to do? Separate from that, and what was happening behind closed doors was, you know, we knew I was pregnant. We now know it's Archie, and it was a boy. We didn't know any of that at the time. We can just talk about it as Archie now. And that was when they were saying they didn't want him to be a prince or a princess — not knowing what the gender would be, which would be different from protocol — and that he wasn't going to receive security.
Oprah: What?
Meghan: It was really hard.
Oprah: What do you mean?
Meghan: He wasn't going to receive security. This went on for the last few months of our pregnancy, where I'm going, 'Hold on a second'.
Oprah: That your son — and Harry, Prince Harry's son was not going to receive security?
Meghan: That's right, I know.
Oprah: How . . . but how does that work?
Meghan: How does that work? It's like, 'No, no, no. Look, because if he's not going to be a prince, it's like, OK, well, he needs to be safe, so we're not saying don't make him a prince or a princess — whatever it's going to be . . . 'But if you're saying the title is what's going to affect their protection, we

haven't created this monster machine around us in terms of clickbait and tabloid fodder. You've allowed that to happen, which means our son needs to be safe'.

Oprah: So, how do they explain to you that your son, the grandson, the great-grandson of the Queen...

Meghan: Mm-hmm.

Oprah: ...is not going to have...he wasn't going to be a prince? How did they tell you that? And what reasons did they give? And then say, 'And so, therefore, you're not...you don't need protection'.

Meghan: There's no explanation. There's no version. I mean, that's the other piece of that...

Oprah: Who tells you that?

Meghan: I heard a lot of it through Harry and then other parts of it through conversations with...

Oprah: Mm-hmm.

Meghan: ...family members. And it was a decision that they felt was appropriate. And I thought, well...

Oprah: Was the title...was him being called a prince, Archie being called a prince, was that important to you?

Meghan: If it meant he was going to be safe, then, of course. All the grandeur surrounding this stuff is an attachment that I don't personally have, right? I've been a waitress, an actress, a princess, a duchess. I've always just still been Meghan, right? So, for me, I'm clear on who I am, independent of all that stuff. And the most important title I will ever have is Mom. I know that.

Meghan: But the idea of our son not being safe, and also the idea of the first member of colour in this family not being titled in the same way that other grandchildren would be...

You know, the other piece of that conversation is, there's a convention — I forget if it was George V or George VI convention — that when you're the grandchild of the monarch, so when Harry's dad becomes king, automatically Archie and our next baby would become prince or princess, or whatever they were going to be.

Oprah: So, for you, it's about protection and safety, not so much as what the ... what the title means to the world.

Meghan: That's a huge piece of it, but, I mean, but ...

Oprah: ... and that having the title gives you the safety and protection?

Meghan: Yeah, but also it's not their right to take it away.

Oprah: Yeah.

Meghan: Right? And so, I think even with that convention I'm talking about, while I was pregnant, they said they want to change the convention for Archie.

Oprah: Mmm.

Meghan: Well, why?

Oprah: Did you get an answer?

Meghan: No.

Oprah: You still don't have an answer?

Meghan: No.

Oprah: You know, we had heard — the world, those of us out here reading the things or hearing the things — that it was you and Harry who didn't want Archie to have a prince title. So, you're telling me that is not true?

Meghan: No, and it's not our decision to make, right?

Oprah: Mm-hmm.

Meghan: ... even though I have a lot of clarity on what comes with the titles, good and bad — and from my

experience, a lot of pain.
Oprah: Mm-hmm.
Meghan: I, again, wouldn't wish pain on my child, but that is their birthright to then make a choice about.
Oprah: OK, so it feels to me like things started to change when you and Harry decided that you were not going to take the picture that had been a part of the tradition for years and...
Meghan: We weren't asked to take a picture. That's also part of the spin, that was really damaging. I thought, 'Can you just tell them the truth? Can you say to the world you're not giving him a title, and we want to keep him safe, and that if he's not a prince, then it's not part of the tradition? Just tell people, and then they'll understand?'
Oprah: Mm-hmm.
Meghan: But they wouldn't do that.
Oprah: But you were... you both, obviously, were aware that had been a part of the tradition? And there was a... was there a specific reason why you didn't want to be a part of that tradition? I think many people interpreted that as you were both saying, 'We're going to do things our way. We're going to do things a different way'.
Meghan: That's not it at all. I mean, I think what was really hard... so, picture, now that you know what was going on behind the scenes, right? There was a lot of fear surrounding it. I was very scared of having to offer up our baby, knowing that they weren't going to be kept safe.
Oprah: You certainly must have had some conversations with Harry about it and have your own suspicions as to why they didn't want to make Archie a prince. What are... what

are those thoughts? Why do you think that is? Do you think it's because of his race?

Meghan: (Sighs)

Oprah: And I know that's a loaded question, but...

Meghan: But I can give you an honest answer. In those months when I was pregnant, all around this same time... so we have in tandem the conversation of 'He won't be given security, he's not going to be given a title' and also concerns and conversations about how dark his skin might be when he's born.

Oprah: What?

Meghan: And...

Oprah: Who... who is having that conversation with you? What?

Meghan: So...

Oprah: There is a conversation... hold on. Hold up. Hold up. Stop right now.

Meghan: There were... there were several conversations about it.

Oprah: There's a conversation with you..?

Meghan: With Harry.

Oprah: About how dark your baby is going to be?

Meghan: Potentially, and what that would mean or look like.

Oprah: Whoo. And you're not going to tell me who had the conversation?

Meghan: I think that would be very damaging to them.

Oprah: OK. So, how... how does one have that meeting?

Meghan: That was relayed to me from Harry. Those were conversations that family had with him. And I think...

Oprah: Whoa.

Meghan: It was really hard to be able to see those as compartmentalised conversations.

Oprah: Because they were concerned that if he were too brown, that that would be a problem? Are you saying that?

Meghan: I wasn't able to follow up with why, but that — if that's the assumption you're making, I think that feels like a pretty safe one, which was really hard to understand, right? Especially when — look, I — the Commonwealth is a huge part of the monarchy, and I lived in Canada, which is a Commonwealth country, for seven years. But it wasn't until Harry and I were together that we started to travel through the Commonwealth, I would say 60 per cent, 70 per cent of which is people of colour, right?

Oprah: Mm-hmm.

Meghan: And growing up as a woman of colour, as a little girl of colour, I know how important representation is. I know how you want to see someone who looks like you in certain positions.

Oprah: Obviously.

Meghan: Even Archie. Like, we read these books, and now he's been — there's one line in one that goes, 'If you can see it, you can be it'. And he goes, 'You can be it!' And I think about that so often, especially in the context of these young girls, but even grown women and men who, when I would meet them in our time in the Commonwealth, how much it meant to them to be able to see someone who looks like them...

Oprah: Mmm.

Meghan: ...in this position. And I could never understand how it wouldn't be seen as an added benefit . . .

Oprah: Mm-hmm.

Meghan: . . . and a reflection of the world today. At all times, but especially right now, to go — 'how inclusive is that, that you can see someone who looks like you in this family, much less one who's born into it?'

(**Oprah** narrates) When Meghan joined the Royal Family in 2018, she became the target of unrelenting, pervasive attacks. Racist abuse online aimed at Meghan Markle. There were undeniable racist overtones. This stands apart from the kind of coverage we've seen of any other royal. There was constant criticism, blatant sexist and racist remarks by British tabloids and internet trolls. We have seen the racism towards her play out in real time. Referring to her as 'straight outta Compton'. The daily onslaught of vitriol and condemnation from the UK Press became overwhelming and, in Meghan's words, 'almost unsurvivable'.

Oprah: You'd said in a podcast that it became 'almost unsurvivable', and that struck me, because it sounds like you were in some kind of mental trouble. What was actually going on? 'Almost unsurvivable' sounds like there was a breaking point.

Meghan: Yeah, there was. I just didn't see a solution. I would sit up at night, and I was just, like, I don't understand how all of this is being churned out. And, again, I wasn't seeing it, but it's almost worse when you feel it through the expression of my mom or my friends, or them calling me crying, just, like, 'Meg, they're not protecting you'. And I realised that it was all happening just because I was breathing. And, look, I was really ashamed to say it at the time and ashamed to have to admit it to Harry, especially, because I know how much loss he's suffered. But I knew that if I didn't say it, that I would do it. And I ... I just didn't ... I just didn't want to be alive any more. And that was a very clear and real and frightening constant thought. And I remember — I remember how he just cradled me. And I was — I went to the institution, and I said that I needed to go somewhere to get help. I said that, 'I've never felt this way before, and I need to go somewhere'. And I was told that I couldn't, that it wouldn't be good for the institution. And I called...

Oprah: So the institution is never a person. Or is it a series of people?

Meghan: No, it's a person.

Oprah: It's a person.

Meghan: It's several people. But I went to one of the most senior people just to ... to get help. And that — you know, I share this, because there's so many people who are afraid to voice that they need help. And I know, personally, how hard it is to not just voice it, but when you voice it, to be told no.

Oprah: Whoo.

Meghan: And so, I went to human resources, and I said, 'I just really — I need help'. Because in my old job, there was a union, and they would protect me. And I remember this conversation like it was yesterday, because they said, 'My heart goes out to you, because I see how bad it is, but there's nothing we can do to protect you because you're not a paid employee of the institution'.

Oprah: Mmm.

Meghan: This wasn't a choice. This was emails and begging for help, saying very specifically, 'I am concerned for my mental welfare'. And people going, 'Oh, yes, yes, it's disproportionately terrible what we see out there to anyone else'. But nothing was ever done, so we had to find a solution.

Oprah: Wow! 'I don't want to be alive any more,' that's . . .

Meghan: I thought it would have solved everything for everyone, right?

Oprah: So, were you thinking of harming yourself? Were you having suicidal thoughts?

Meghan: Yes. This was very, very clear.

Oprah: Wow.

Meghan: Very clear and very scary. And, you know, I didn't know who to even turn to in that. And one of the people that I reached out to, who's continued to be a friend and confidant, was one of my husband's mom's best friends, one of Diana's best friends. Because it's, like, who else could understand what's . . . what it's actually like on the inside?

Oprah: Did you ever think about going to a hospital? Or is that possible, that you can check yourself in some place?

Meghan: No, that's what I was asking to do.

Oprah: Yeah.

Meghan: You can't just do that. I couldn't, you know, call an Uber to the palace.

Oprah: Yeah.

Meghan: You couldn't just go. You couldn't. I mean, you have to understand, as well, when I joined that family, that was the last time, until we came here, that I saw my passport, my driver's licence, my keys. All that gets turned over. I didn't see any of that any more.

Oprah: Well, the way you're describing this, it... it's like you were trapped and couldn't get help, even though you're on the verge of suicide. That's what you are describing. That's what I'm hearing.
Meghan: Yes.
Oprah: And that would be an accurate interpretation, yes?
Meghan: That's the truth.
Oprah: That's the truth.
Meghan: You know, and if you think about... it was one of the things that... it stills haunts me is this photograph that someone had sent me. We had to go to an official event. We had to go to this event at the Royal Albert Hall, and a friend said, 'I know you don't look at pictures, but, oh, my God, you guys look so great...'
Oprah: Yeah.
Meghan: ... and sent it to me. And I zoomed in, and what I saw was the truth of what that moment was, because right before we had to leave for that, I had just had that conversation with Harry that morning, and it was the next day that I talked to the institution.
Oprah: You had the conversation 'I don't want to be alive any more'?
Meghan: Yeah.
Oprah: Whoo.
Meghan: No, and it was... it wasn't even, 'I don't want to'.
Oprah: And then, you..?
Meghan: It was like, 'These are the thoughts that I'm having in the middle of the night that are very clear...'
Oprah: Yes, clarification.
Meghan: '... and I'm scared, because this is very real. This

isn't some abstract idea. This is methodical, and this is not who I am'. But we had to go to this event, and I remember him saying, 'I don't think you can go'. And I said, 'I can't be left alone'.

Oprah: Because you were afraid of what you might do to yourself?

Meghan: And we went, and that...

Oprah: I'm so sorry to hear that.

Meghan: ... and that picture, if you zoom in, what I see is how tightly his knuckles are gripped around mine. You can see the whites of our knuckles, because we are smiling and doing our job, but we're both just trying to hold on. And every time that those lights went down in that Royal Box, I was just weeping, and he was gripping my hand.

Oprah: Wow.

Meghan: And then, it was, 'OK, intermission's coming, the lights are about to come on, everyone's looking at us again', and you have to just be on again.

Oprah: Yeah.

Meghan: And that's, I think, so important for people to remember is you have no idea what's going on for someone behind closed doors. You have no idea. Even the people that smile the biggest smiles and shine the brightest lights, it seems, to have compassion for what's actually potentially going on.

Oprah: I know. The public is looking at you. And to think that you, earlier in the day, had said to Harry that you didn't want to be alive any more.

Meghan: Yeah. And just hours before, just sitting on the... the steps in our cottage... just sitting there and then going, 'ok, well, go upstairs and put your make-up bag in your sink and try to pull yourself together'.

Oprah: Nobody should have to go through that.

Meghan: And, you know, Harry and I are working on this mental health series for Apple, and we — yes, so — we, we, we hear a lot of these stories. Nobody should have to go through that. It takes so much courage to admit that you need help.

Oprah: Mm-hmm.

Meghan: It takes so much courage to voice that. And as I said, I was ashamed. I'm supposed to be stronger than that.

Oprah: Mm-hmm.

Meghan: I don't want to put more on my husband's shoulders. He's carrying the weight of the world. I don't want to bring that to him. I bring solutions. To admit that you need help, to admit how dark of a place you're in.

Oprah: You've said some pretty shocking things here, revealing...

Meghan: I wasn't planning to say anything shocking.

Oprah: OK.

Meghan: I'm just telling you what's happened.

Oprah: OK.

Meghan: I'm sorry if it's shocked you! It's been a lot.

Oprah: I'm a little shocked.

Meghan: It's been a lot.

Oprah: How do you feel about the palace hearing you speak your truth today? Are you afraid of a backlash or their reaction?

Meghan: I mean, I think I'm not going to live my life in fear. You know, I think so much of it is said with an understanding of just truth.

Oprah: Mm-hmm.

Meghan: But I think, to answer your question, I don't know how they could expect that after all of this time, we would still just be silent if there is an active role that The Firm is playing in perpetuating falsehoods about us.

Oprah: Mmm.

Meghan: That at a certain point, you're going to go, 'But, you guys, someone just tell the truth'. And if that comes with risk of losing things, I mean, I've lost... there's a lot that's been lost already. Now she is expecting her second child and says she knows life is worth living

Meghan: And I grieve a lot. I mean, I've lost my father. I lost a baby. I nearly lost my name. I mean, there's the loss of identity. But I'm still standing, and my hope for people in the takeaway from this is to know that there's another side.

Oprah: Mm-hmm.

Meghan: To know that life is worth living.

Oprah: OK. I'm so glad you see that now. We are going to take a break, y'all, and Harry's going to join us.

Oprah: So, hi.

Harry: Hello.

Oprah: Thanks for joining us.

Harry: Thanks for having me.

Oprah: You've been watching on the side, yeah?

Harry: Some of it.

Oprah: Yes. I want to say, first of all, let's say congratulations...

Harry: Thank you.

Oprah: ... for the new addition to your family. Meghan said

she wanted to wait until you were here to tell us, is it a boy or is it a girl?
Meghan: You can tell her.
Harry: No, go for it.
Meghan: No, no.
Harry: It's a girl.
Meghan: It's a girl.
Harry: Yes!
Oprah: You're going to have a daughter. Wow.
Meghan: It's a girl.
Oprah: When you realised that and saw it on the ultrasound, what... what... what was your first thought?
Harry: Amazing. Just grateful, like any — to have any child, any one or any two would have been amazing. But to have a boy and then a girl, you know, what more can you ask for? But now, you know, now we — we've got our family. We've got, you know, the four of us and our two dogs, and it's great.
Oprah: Done. Done? Two is it?
Harry: Done.
Meghan: Two is it.
Oprah: Two is it.
Meghan: Two is it.
Oprah: And when's the baby due?
Meghan: In summertime.
Oprah: This summertime?
Meghan: Yeah.
Oprah: So, you all have been living in sunny California now for...
Meghan: Since March.

Oprah: Since March, OK.

(**Oprah** narrates) In late 2019, Prince Harry and Meghan left the UK And moved to Canada. The couple says they chose Canada, a commonwealth of Britain, with the intention of continuing to serve the Queen. After their move, Harry and Meghan say security normally provided by the Royal Family was cut off. By March 2020, just days before the Covid lockdown began, Meghan, Harry and Archie relocated to Los Angeles, where media mogul Tyler Perry offered them his home as a temporary refuge. He also provided security.

Three months later they bought their own home and settled in the Santa Barbara area. Last spring, the Duke and Duchess of Sussex created their own foundation and media content company called Archewell.

Harry: Three months, I believe.

Meghan: Yeah, because we didn't have a plan. We needed ... we needed a house and he offered security as well, so it gave us breathing room to try to figure out what we are going to do.

Harry: The biggest concern was that while we were in Canada, in someone else's house, I then got told at short notice security was going to be removed. By this point, courtesy of the Daily Mail, the world knew exact ... our exact location. So suddenly it dawned on me, 'Hang on a second. The borders could be closed. We're going to have our security removed. Who knows how long lockdown's going to be? The world knows where we are. It's not safe. It's not secure'.

Meghan: Well, and also ...

Harry: We probably need to get out of here.

Oprah: So, what security did you have at the time that was going to be removed?

Harry: We had our UK security.

Oprah: So you got word from overseas?

Harry: Yeah.

Oprah: That 'we're taking away your security'. Why were they doing that?

Harry: Their justification is a change in status, of which I pushed back and said, 'Well, is there a change of threat or risk?' And after many weeks of waiting, eventually I got the confirmation that no, the risk and threat hasn't changed but due to our change of status, (by) which we would no longer be official working members of the Royal Family, they're obviously... what we proposed was sort of part-time, or at least as much as we could do without being fully consumed because of, I think, what most of you guys have covered already.

Meghan: We actually didn't talk about that. It's been so spun in the wrong direction, as though we quit, we walked away, we... all the conversations of the two years before we finally announced it.

(**Oprah** narrates) In January 2020, Prince Harry and Meghan announced they would step back as senior members of the Royal Family. The swiftness with which they've taken this decision, only 18 months after they got married, has taken everyone by surprise, from the Queen all the way down.

The bombshell news sparked a worldwide media frenzy dubbed 'Megxit' by the British Press. Many reporters and viral posts blamed Meghan for the decision. In an official statement, Queen Elizabeth said: 'Although we would have preferred them to remain full-time working members of the Royal Family, we respect and understand their wish to live a more independent life as a family while remaining a valued part of my family.' (Back to **Oprah**)

Oprah: OK, let me ask the question.

Meghan: Yeah?

Oprah: So, over a year ago, you shocked the world. You announced you were stepping back as senior members of the Royal Family. And then the media reported that you had 'blindsided' the Queen, your grandmother. So here's a time to set the record straight. What was the tipping point that made you decide you had to leave?

Harry: Yeah, it was desperate. I went to all the places which I thought I should go to, to ask for help. We both did.

Meghan: Mm-hmm.

Harry: Separately and together.

Oprah: So you left because you were asking for help and couldn't get it?

Harry: Yeah, basically. But we never left.

Meghan: We never left the family and we only wanted to have the same type of role that exists, right? There's senior members of the family and then there are non-senior members. And we said, specifically, 'We're stepping back from senior roles to be just like several...' I mean, I can think of so many right now who are all...they're royal highnesses, prince or princess, duke or duchess...who earn a living, live on palace grounds, can support the Queen if and when called upon. So we weren't reinventing the wheel here. We were saying, 'OK, if this isn't working for everyone, we're in a lot of pain, you can't provide us with the help we need, we can just take a step back. We can do it in a Commonwealth country'. We suggested New Zealand, South Africa...

Harry: Take a breath.

Meghan: Canada.

Oprah: Yeah. And you wanted to take a breath from what specifically? Let's be clear.

Harry: From this... this constant barrage. My biggest concern was history repeating itself and I've said that before on numerous occasions, very publicly. And what I was seeing was history repeating itself. But more, perhaps. Or definitely far more dangerous because then you add race in and you add social media in. And when I'm talking about history repeating itself, I'm talking about my... my mother.

Harry: When you can see something happening in the same kind of way, anybody would ask for help, ask the system of which you are a part of — especially when you know there's a relationship there — that they could help and share some truth or call... call the dogs off, whatever you want to call it. So to receive no help at all and to be told continuously, 'This is how it is. This is just how it is. We've all been through it'... and I think the biggest turning point for me was the... and it didn't take very long. It was actually right at the beginning ... was, OK, this union ... us, me, being ... having a girlfriend was going to be a thing. Of course it was. But I... I never expected, or I never thought...

Oprah: Because she was mixed race?

Harry: No, just... just the two of us to start with. I hadn't really thought about the mixed-race piece because I thought, well... well, firstly, you know, I've spent many years doing the work and doing my own learning. But my upbringing in the system, of which I was brought up in and what I've been exposed to, it wasn't... I wasn't aware of it to start with. But, my god, it doesn't take very long to suddenly become aware of it.

Oprah: Yeah, because you said you really weren't aware of unconscious bias and all that that represents...

Harry: No.

Oprah: Until you met Meghan.

Harry: Yeah. You know, as sad as it is to say, it takes living in her shoes — in this instance, for a day, or those first eight days — to see where it was going to go and how far they were going to take it.

Oprah: And get away with it?

Harry: And get away with it and be so blatant about it. That's the bit that shocked me. This is... we're talking about the UK Press here, right? And this... the UK is my home. That is... that is where I was brought up. So yes, I've got my own relationship that goes back a long way with the media. I asked for calm from the British tabloids — once as a boyfriend, once as a husband and once as a father.

Oprah: So when I ask the question, 'Why did you leave?' the simplest answer is..?

Harry: Lack of support and lack of understanding.

Oprah: So, I want clarity. Was the move about getting away from the UK Press? Because the Press, as you know, is everywhere. Or was the move because you weren't getting enough support from The Firm?

Harry: It was both.

Oprah: Both.

Harry: Yeah.
Oprah: Did you blindside the Queen?
Harry: No. I've never blindsided my grandmother. I have too much respect for her.
Oprah: So where did that story come from?
Harry: I hazard a guess that it probably could have come from within the institution.
Oprah: Mmm.
Meghan: So, I remember when you talked to her several times about this over...
Harry: Two years.
Meghan: Two years. But even the night before, days before, with the statement coming out, I remember that conversation.
Oprah: So, how do you know she wasn't blindsided? Because the way it was presented through the Press is that suddenly you made this announcement. She didn't know it was coming.
Harry insisted the Queen wasn't blindsided by MegxitCredit: AFP or licensors
Harry: No, I... when we were in Canada, I had three conversations with my grandmother and two conversations with my father and — before he stopped taking my calls — and he said, 'Can you put this all in writing what your plan is?'
Oprah: Your father asked you to put it in writing.
Harry: Yeah. He asked me to put it in writing and I put all the specifics in there, even the fact that we were planning on putting the announcement out on January 7.
Oprah: So you just said that your dad stopped taking your

calls. Why did he stop taking your calls?

Harry: Because I took matters in...by that point, I took matters into my own hands. It was like, 'I need to do this for my family. This is not a surprise to anybody. It's really sad that it's gotten to this point but I've got to do something for my own mental health, my wife's and for Archie's as well'. Because I could see where this was headed.

Meghan: To have sat back and not said that for so long, it just feels really...

Oprah: To have been silenced all this time.

Meghan: Yeah.

Harry: Been three and a half, four years. Or longer, actually.

Meghan: We were saying...gosh, it must have been years ago we were sitting in Nottingham (Nottingham Cottage, where Harry lived as a bachelor and when first married)...I was sitting in Nottingham Cottage and The Little Mermaid came on. Now, who watches...who as an adult really watches The Little Mermaid? But it came on and I was like, 'Well, I'm just here all the time, so I may as well watch this'. And I went, 'Oh, my god! She falls in love with the prince and because of that, she has to lose her voice'.

Oprah: Mmm.

Meghan: But by the end, she gets her voice back.

Oprah: Gets her voice back.

Meghan: Yeah.

Oprah: And this is what happened here? You feel like you got your voice back?

Meghan: Yeah.

Oprah: So, you...you're stepping back out of frustration and you just need to get out. And, you know, you heard

Meghan share with us all...
Harry: Mm-hmm.
Oprah: The moment that she came to you, had the courage enough to say out loud...
Harry: Mm-hmm.
Oprah: 'I don't want to live any more.'
Harry: Mm-hmm.
Oprah: And you didn't know what to do?
Harry: I had no idea what to do. I wasn't...I wasn't prepared for that. I went...I went to a very dark place as well. But I...I wanted to be there for her and...
Meghan: Also, we didn't leave right that minute, right?
Harry: I was terrified.
Meghan: We still...that's almost a year after.
Oprah: So then did you tell other people in the family, 'I have to get help for her. We need help for her'?
Harry: No. That's just not a conversation that would be had.
Oprah: Why?
Harry: I guess I was ashamed of admitting it to them.
Oprah: Oh.
Harry: And I don't know whether...I don't know whether they've had the same...whether they've had the same feelings or thoughts. I have no idea. And it's a very trapping environment that a lot of them are stuck in.
Oprah: You were ashamed of admitting that Meghan needed help?
Harry: Yeah.
Oprah: Mmm.
Harry: I didn't have anyone to turn to.
Oprah: Mm-hmm.

Harry: You know, we've got some very close friends that... that have been with us through this whole process but for the family, they very much have this mentality of, 'This is just how it is. This is how it's meant to be. You can't change it. We've all been through it'.

Oprah: 'We've all been through the pressure. We've all been through being exploited'?

Harry: Yes. But what was different for me was the race element, because now it wasn't just about her, but it is about what she represents. And therefore it wasn't just affecting my wife. It was affecting so many other people as well. And that's... that was the trigger for me to really engage in those conversations with Palace... senior Palace staff and with my family to say, 'Guys, this is not going to end well'.

Oprah: And when you say 'end well', what did you mean?

Harry: For anyone it's not going to end well. Because the way that I saw it was there was a way of doing things but for us — for this union and the specifics around her race — there was an opportunity, many opportunities, for my family to show some public support.

Oprah: Mmm.

Harry: And I guess one of the most telling parts — and the saddest parts, I guess — was over 70 Members of Parliament, female Members of Parliament, both Conservative and Labour — came out and called out the... the colonial undertones of articles and headlines written about

Meghan. Yet no one from my family ever said anything over those three years. And that ... that hurts. But I also am acutely aware of where my family stand and how scared they are of the tabloids turning on them.

Oprah: Turning on them for what? They're the Royal Family.

Harry: Yes, but it's... there is this invisible... what's termed or referred to as the 'invisible contract' behind closed doors between the institution and the tabloids, the UK tabloids.

Oprah: How so?

Harry: Well, it is... to simplify it, it's a case of if you... if you as a family member are willing to wine, dine and give full access to these reporters, then you will get better press.

Oprah: What do you care about better press if you're royal?

Harry: I think everyone needs to have some compassion for... for them in that situation, right? There is a level of control by fear that has existed for generations. I mean, generations.

Oprah: But who's controlling whom? It's the institution. From our point of view, just the public. It's...

Harry: Yeah but the institution survives based on that, on that perception. So actually, if you don't...

Oprah: So you're saying there's this relationship that **Meghan** was speaking of... it's like, symbiotic. One lives or thrives because the other exists.

Meghan: Mmm.

Oprah: That's what you're saying.

Harry: That's the... that's the idea.

Meghan: Well, see, I think there's a reason that these tabloids have holiday parties at the Palace. They're hosted by the Palace, the tabloids are. You know, there is a construct that's at play there. And because from the beginning of our relationship, they were so attacking and inciting so much racism, really, it changed our... the risk level, because it went... it wasn't just catty gossip. It was bringing out a part of people that was racist in how it was charged. And that changed the threat. That changed the level of death threats. That changed everything.

Oprah: So, tell me this: You said a moment ago, it hurts that your family has never acknowledged the role that racism played in here. Did you think she was well received in the beginning?

Harry: Yes. Far better than I expected. (Laughter) But, you know, my grandmother has been amazing throughout. You know, my father, my brother, Kate and... and all the rest of the family, they were, they were really welcoming. But it really changed after the Australia tour, after our South Pacific tour.

Meghan: That's when we announced we were pregnant with Archie. That was our first tour.

Harry: But it was also... it was also the first time that the family got to see how incredible she is at the job. And that brought back memories.

Oprah: I'm thinking, because I watch The Crown OK? I watch The Crown. Do you all watch The Crown?

Meghan: (Laughs)

Harry:: I've watched some of it. You've watched some of it?

Meghan: I've watched some of it.

Oprah: But there's this... I think it was the fourth season, actually, where there is an Australian tour. So, is that what you're talking about? It brought back memories of that? The Australian tour.

Harry: Yeah.

Oprah: Where your father and your mother went there, and your mother was bedazzling. So, are you saying that there were hints of jealousy?

Harry: Look, I just wish that we would all learn from the past. But to see the...to see how effortless it was for **Meghan** to come into the family so quickly in Australia and across New Zealand, Fiji and Tonga, and just be able to connect with people in such a...

Oprah: But...

Harry: I know, I know, I know, I know. But it's...

Oprah: Why, I mean, why wouldn't everybody love that? Isn't that what you want? You want her to come into the family and to, as the Queen said at one point, the way that Meghan had basically, not her words, been assimilated into the family.

Harry: Yeah, I think, you know, as we talked about, she was very much welcomed into the family, not just by the family, but by the world.

Oprah: Yeah.

Harry: Certainly by the Commonwealth. I mean, here you have one of the greatest assets to the Commonwealth that the family could have ever wished for.

Oprah: I just can't...I'm kind of going back to this. So, then, you're in Canada because you had stepped back. Your Firm says you're no longer going to have protection. So, did you ask for that? Because did you want...were you trying to have it both ways? You wanted to step back but also keep your foot in royal business, it seems.

Harry: It's interesting that you talk about it being, you know, 'Have it both ways' on the...on the security element. I never thought that I would have my security removed, because I was born into this position. I inherited the risk. So that was a shock to me. That was what completely changed the whole plan.

Oprah: So, that you as Prince Harry are going to have your security removed.

Meghan: Yeah. And I even ... and I even wrote letters to his family saying, 'Please, it's very clear the protection of me or Archie is not a priority. I accept that. That is fine. Please keep my husband safe. I see the death threats. I see the racist propaganda. Please keep him safe. Please don't pull his security and announce to the world when he and we are most vulnerable'. And they said it's just not possible.

Oprah: Mm-hmm. I think what we really have got to clear up here is because one of the stories that continues to live, either through rumours or social media, out in the world, is that you, Meghan, are the one who manipulated, calculated, and are responsible for this Megxit.

Meghan: Oh, my gosh. It's amazing how they can use Meg for everything.

Oprah: Yes. There are even stories that you knew all along that this was going to happen. You went through the whole process, and it was all intentional to build your brand.

Meghan: Can you imagine how little sense that makes? I left my career, my life. I left everything because I love him, right? And our plan was to do this for ever.

Harry: Yes.

Meghan: Our plan ... for me, I mean, I wrote letters to his family when I got there, saying, 'I am dedicated to this. I'm here for you. Use me as you'd like'. There was no guidance, as well, right? There were certain things that you couldn't do. But, you know, unlike what you see in the movies, there's no class on how to... how to speak, how to cross your legs, how to be royal. There's none of that training. That might exist for other members of the family. That was not something that was offered to me.

Oprah: So, nobody tells you anything?

Meghan: No.

Oprah: Nobody prepares you?

Meghan: Nobody even...

Harry: There's...

Meghan: Sorry, but even down to, like, the National Anthem. No one thought to say, 'Oh, you're American. You're not going to know that'. That's me late at night, Googling how... what's the National... I've got to learn this. I don't want to embarrass them. I need to learn these 30 hymns for church. All of this is televised. We were doing the training behind the scenes, because I just wanted to make them proud.

Oprah: OK, but here's the question: Do you think you would have left or ever stepped back were it not for Meghan?

Meghan: Hm.

Harry: No. The answer to your question is no.

Oprah: You would not have?

Harry: I wouldn't have... I wouldn't have been able to, because I myself was trapped as well. I didn't see a way out.

Oprah: She felt trapped, you were trapped?

Harry: Yeah, I didn't see a way out.

Oprah: But you'd this life, your whole life. This has been your life your whole life.

Harry: Yeah, but, you know, I was trapped, but I didn't know

I was trapped.

Oprah: Mmm.

Harry: But the moment that I met Meg, and then our worlds sort of collided in the most amazing of ways, and then to see how...

Oprah: Please explain how you, Prince Harry, raised in a palace and a life of privilege — literally, a Prince... how you were trapped.

Harry: Trapped within the system, like the rest of my family are. My father and my brother, they are trapped. They don't get to leave. And I have huge compassion for that.

Oprah: Well, OK, so the impression of the world — maybe it's a false impression — is that, for all these years before **Meghan**, you were living your life as a royal, Prince **Harry**... the beloved Prince Harry and that you were enjoying that life. We didn't get the impression that you were feeling trapped in that life.

Harry: Enjoying the life because there were photographs of me smiling while I was shaking hands and meeting people? Like, I'm sure you guys have covered some of that. That's... that's a part of the job. That's a part of the role. That's what's expected. No matter who you are in the family, no matter what's going on in your personal life, no matter what's just happened, if the bikes roll up and the car rolls up, you've got to get dressed, you got to get in there. You wipe your tears away, shake off whatever you're thinking about and you got to be on your A-game.

Oprah: Mm-hmm. What would you think your mum would say about this stepping back, this decision to step back from the Royal Family? How would she feel about this moment?

Harry: I think she would feel very angry with how this has panned out, and very sad. But, ultimately, she'd... all she'd... all she'd ever want is for us to be happy.

Oprah: You wanted freedom from... from that life? You wanted freedom to make your own money. You wanted freedom to make deals with Netflix and Spotify. But you also wanted to serve the Queen?

Harry: Yeah, we didn't want to... we didn't want to give up, or we didn't want to turn our backs on the associations and the people that we ... that we've been supporting.

Meghan: But also, Oprah, it exists.

Harry: Yeah, it exists. But, also, the Netflix and the Spotify, they're all... that was never part of the plan.

Meghan: Yeah.

Oprah: Because you didn't have a plan?

Meghan: We didn't have a plan.

Harry: We didn't have a plan. That was suggested by somebody else by the point of where my family literally cut me off financially, and I had to afford... afford security for us.

Oprah: Wait. Hold... hold up. Wait a minute. Your family cut you off?

Harry: Yeah, in the first half, the first quarter of 2020. But I've got what my mum left me, and, without that, we would not have been able to do this.

Oprah: OK.

Harry: So, you know, touching back on what you asked me, what my mum would think of this, I think she saw it coming. And I certainly felt her presence throughout this whole process. And, you know, for me, I'm... I'm just really relieved and happy to be sitting here talking to you with my wife by my side. Because I can't begin to imagine what it must have been like for her going through this process by herself all those years ago, because it's been unbelievably tough for the two of us, but at least we had each other.

Oprah: What's your relationship like now with your family?

Harry: I've spoken more to my grandmother in the last year than I have done for many, many years.

Oprah: Do you all have Zoom calls?

Harry: We did a couple of Zoom calls with Archie.

Meghan: Sometimes, yes, so they can see Archie.

Oprah: Yeah.

Harry: My grandmother and I have a really good relationship...

Oprah: Mm-hmm.

Harry: ...And an understanding. And I have a deep respect for her. She's my Colonel-In-Chief, right? She always will be.

Oprah: Your relationship with your father? Is he taking your calls now?

Harry: Yeah. Yeah, he is. There's a lot to work through there, you know? I feel really let down, because he's been through something similar. He knows what pain feels like, and this is...and Archie's his grandson. And...but, at the same time, you know, I, of course I will always...I will always love him, but there's a lot of hurt that's happened. And...and I will continue to...to make it one of my priorities to try and heal that relationship. And, but they only know what they know, and that's the thing. I've tried to...

Meghan: Or what they're told.

Harry: Or what they're told. And I've tried to educate them

through the process that I have been educated.
Oprah: Because is it like being in a big royal bubble?
Harry: Yeah.
Oprah: Yeah. And your brother? Relationship? Much has been said about that.
Harry: Yeah, and much will continue to be said about that. You know, as I've said before, I love William to bits. He's my brother. We've been through hell together. I mean, we have a shared experience. But we... you know, we're on... we're on different paths.
Oprah: Well, what is particularly striking is what Meghan shared with us earlier, is that no one wants to admit that there's anything about race or that race has played a role in the trolling and the vitriol, and yet Meghan shared with us that there was a conversation with you about Archie's skin tone.
Harry: Mm-hmm.
Oprah: What was that conversation?
Harry: That conversation I'm never going to share, but at the time... at the time, it was awkward. I was a bit shocked.
Oprah: Can you... can you tell us what the question was?
Harry: No. I don't... I'm not comfortable with sharing that.
Oprah: OK.
Harry: But that was... that was right at the beginning, right?
Oprah: Like, what will the baby look like?
Harry: Yeah, what will the kids look like?
Oprah: What will the kids look like?
Harry: But that was right at the beginning, when she wasn't going to get security, when members of my family were

suggesting that she carries on acting, because there was not enough money to pay for her, and all this sort of stuff. Like, there was some real obvious signs before we even got married that this was going to be really hard.

Oprah: So, in conclusion, if you'd had the support, you'd still be there?

Harry: Without question.

Meghan: Yeah.

Harry: I'm sad that ... that what's happened has happened, but I know, and I'm comfortable in knowing, that we did everything that we could to make it work. And we did everything on the exit process the way that ... the way that it should have been done.

Meghan: With as much respect.

Harry: With as much respect.

Meghan: And, oh, my God, we just did everything we could to ... to protect them.

Oprah: So, what do you say to the people who say you came here, you made these multimillion-dollar deals and that you're just money-grabbing royals?

Harry: First off, this was never the intention.

Oprah: Mm-hmm.

Meghan: Yeah.

Harry: And we're certainly not complaining. We ... our life is great now. We've got a beautiful house. We've got a beautiful ... I've got a beautiful family. And the dogs ... the dogs are really happy. But at the time, during Covid, the suggestion by a friend was, 'What about streamers?'

Meghan: Yeah, we genuinely hadn't thought about that before.

Harry: We hadn't thought about it. So there were all sorts of different options. And, look, from my perspective, all I needed was enough money to be able to pay for security to keep my family safe.

Oprah: Mm. How will you use Archewell as a means of speaking to things that are important to you in the world?

Meghan: I think in creating... I mean, life is about storytelling, right? About the stories we tell ourselves, the stories we're told, what we buy into. And... and for us to be able to have storytelling through a truthful lens, that hopefully is uplifting, is going to be great knowing how many people that can land with. And being able to give a voice to a lot of people that are under-represented and aren't really heard.

Oprah: Any regrets?

Meghan: This morning, I woke up earlier than H and saw a note from someone on our team in the UK saying the Duke of Edinburgh had gone to the hospital.

Oprah: Yeah.

Meghan: But I just picked up the phone and I called the Queen just to check in.

Oprah: You check in?

Meghan: Just like, I would... you know... that's what we do. It's like, being able to default to not having to every moment go, 'Is that appropriate?'

Oprah: Yeah.

Harry: For so many in my family, what they do is... there's a level of control in it, right? Because they're fearful of what the papers are going to say about them.

Oprah: Yeah.

Harry: Whereas with us, it was just, like, just be... just be yourself. Just be genuine. Just be authentic. Just go and do what it is. If you get it wrong, you get it wrong. If you get it right, you get it right.

(**Oprah** narrates) On February 19, 2021, Buckingham palace released a statement announcing it was agreed that Prince Harry and Meghan would not return as working members of the Royal Family. Harry and Meghan's royal patronages and Prince Harry's honorary military titles would be returned to the Queen. The Queen's statement was released after our interview took place. (Back to **Oprah**)

Oprah: Your exit agreement with the Royal Family, it's... that is coming up at the end of this month.

Harry: The decision is, I think. Yeah, I mean, the decision — what, as of last week, or whatever it was — is that they will be removing everything.

Oprah: Are you hurt by that decision?

Harry: I am hurt. But at the same time I completely respect my grandmother's decision. I would still love for us to be able to continue to support those associations, albeit without the title or the role.

Oprah: Could you be as satisfied now, doing this through your own organisation, Archewell?

Meghan: Well, we... this is what we're doing, right? We're still doing it. We're still going to always do the work. But I also think it's important for you or everyone to know this decision that was made about patronages and all of that was before anyone knew that we were sitting down with you.

Harry: Yeah.

Meghan: I think that it's... I can only imagine...

Oprah: I heard a story that you're getting punished now. Those were being taken away because you did sit down with me.

Meghan: Yeah, but that was... those letters, those conversations, that was... that was finalised before anyone even knew that we were going to sit down. So that's just not true.

Oprah: All right, tell me this. Harry, what delights you now in your everyday experience and the things that you actually cherish in your life here with Archie and Meghan?

Harry: This year has been crazy for everybody. But to have outdoor space where I can go for walks with Archie, and we can go for walks as a family and with the dogs, and we can go on hikes — we'll go down to the beach, which is so close — all of these things are just... I guess, the highlight for me is sticking him on the back of the bicycle in his little baby seat and taking him on these bike rides, which is something I was never able to do when I was young. I can see him on the back and he's got his arms out and he's like, 'Whoo!' chatting, chatting, chatting, going, 'Palm tree! House!' and all this sort of stuff. And I do... I think to myself...

Oprah: What's his new favourite word? What's his favourite word now?

Meghan: Oh my gosh, he's on a roll. In the past couple weeks it has been hydrate, which is just hysterical.

Harry: But also, whenever everyone leaves the house, he's like, 'Drive safe'.

Meghan: 'Drive safe'.

Harry: Which is really...

Meghan: He's not even two yet!

Oprah: You said that your brother was trapped. You said that you love your brother and always will love your brother. You didn't tell me what the relationship is now, though.

Harry: The relationship is space at the moment. And, you know, time heals all things, hopefully.

Oprah: Any regrets?

Harry: No. I mean... no, I think we've done... I'm really proud of us, you know? I'm so proud of... I'm so proud of my wife. Like, she safely delivered Archie during a period of time which was so cruel and so mean. And every single day, I was coming back from work, from London, I was coming back to my wife crying while breastfeeding Archie. That's coming from someone who wasn't reading anything. And as she touched on earlier, if she had read anything, she wouldn't be here now. So we did what we had to do — and now we've got another little one on the way.

Meghan: I have one. My regret is believing them when they said I would be protected. I believed that. And I regret believing that because I think, 'had I really seen that that wasn't happening, I would have been able to do more'. But I think I wasn't supposed to see it. I wasn't supposed to know. And... and now, because we're actually on the other side, we've actually not just survived but are thriving. You know, this... I mean, this is miracles. I... yeah, I think that all of those things that I was hoping for have happened... and this is in some ways just the beginning for us. You know, we've been through a lot. It's felt like a lifetime. (Laughs.) A lifetime.

Oprah: So, your story with the prince does have a happy ending?

Meghan: It does.
Harry: Yeah.
Meghan: Yeah. (Laughs.) It really did.
Oprah: It has a happy ending because you made it so.
Meghan: Yeah, greater than any fairytale you've ever read.
Oprah: Greater than any fairytale.
Meghan: Yeah, yeah.
Oprah: What you've described here today — being trapped and not even being aware of it and all the things that had transpired, and then she comes into your life and then you're doing therapy — do you think in some way she saved you?
Harry: Yeah. Without question. There was... there was a bigger purpose. There was other forces at play, I think, throughout this whole process. I'm the last person to think, 'Ooh!' You know? But it's undeniable when these things have happened, where the overlap is. So yeah, she did. Without question she saved me.
Meghan: And I would... I would... I mean, I think that's lovely. I would disagree. I think he saved all of us, right? He ultimately called it and was like, 'We've got to find a way for us, for Archie'. And you made a decision that saved... certainly saved my life and saved all of us. But, you know, you need to want to be saved.
Oprah: Well, thank you for sharing your love story. We can't wait for the big day some time this summer.
Meghan: Yes, indeed.
Oprah: Sometime this summer.
Meghan: Yeah.
Oprah: Thank you both for trusting me to share your story.

****

REFERENCES
1. East Anglian Daily Times 13/12/22
2. YouPol, sample 459 18+ yr olds, 15/01/23
3. Financial Times online 16/09/22
4. 'REPUBLIC' website 4/11/22
5. 'Prince Andrew's Royal Protection Cop Reveals All: Paul Page' / True Crime Podcast 75 –You Tube, 2022

DON'T FORGET TO LEAVE A REVIEW!
Dear Reader,
If you have enjoyed reading this book, why not leave a revue? Your opinion is important to me, and can be a great help to others who are thinking of buying this book...
Best wishes – Roland Gough

ALSO BY ROLAND GOUGH:

ROYAL FAMILY ROYAL SCANDAL

A definitive account of how royal scandals of the past few years have rocked the Royal Family to its very foundations...